We Love to Sew

BEDROOMS

Cool Stuff for Your Space

⫸⟶ 23 Projects ⟵⫷

Annabel Wrigley

FunStitch
S T U D I O
stitch your art out.

Publisher: Amy Marson

Creative Director: Gailen Runge

Art Director/Book Designer: Kristy Zacharias

Editors: Liz Aneloski and Lee Jonsson

Technical Editors: Nanette S. Zeller, Carolyn Aune, and Teresa Stroin

Production Coordinator: Jenny Davis

Production Editor: Alice Mace Nakanishi

Illustrator: Jessica Jenkins

Photography by Kristen Gardner, unless otherwise noted

Published by Fun Stitch Studio, an imprint of C&T Publishing, Inc., P.O. Box 1456, Lafayette, CA 94549

Library of Congress Cataloging-in-Publication Data

Wrigley, Annabel, 1972-

We love to sew--bedrooms : 23 projects : cool stuff for your space / Annabel Wrigley.

pages cm

Audience: Age 8 to 14.

ISBN 978-1-60705-824-3 (soft cover)

1. Sewing--Juvenile literature. 2. Girls' bedrooms--Juvenile literature. 3. Interior decoration--Juvenile literature. 4. Textile crafts--Juvenile literature. 5. Handicraft for girls--Juvenile literature. I. Title. II. Title: Bedrooms.

TT712.W76 2014

646.2'04--dc23

2013028856

Printed in China

10 9 8 7 6 5 4 3 2 1

Dedication

For my students

♥

Acknowledgments

Writing this book has been such a fun experience for me, made even more enjoyable by the amazing support and help of my wonderful family.

To my friends, who helped me with constant encouragement, support, and creative vision. I love that you all stuck by me during my months of work. Thanks to Alessandra, who was not only an amazing help but also the best studio partner a girl could ask for.

To Roxane Cerda, my super awesome editor who told me that I absolutely could manage another book and whose guidance and patience were invaluable. I am so thrilled to call you my friend.

To my amazing book team, Liz, Kristy, Nanette, and everyone at C&T. Thank you all for helping me make another beautiful book.

To Kristen Gardner, my fabulous photographer. Once again you have helped make my book look more beautiful than I could have ever imagined!

Of course, I would not be here without my wonderful group of enthusiastic young students. You make me excited to get out of bed each day and create with you!

Contents

PROJECTS

A Message from Denyse Schmidt

I was very fortunate to grow up in a family where making useful and beautiful things was second nature. There wasn't anything my parents wouldn't—or couldn't—try. With a trusty old heavy-duty sewing machine, my parents taught themselves to reupholster by practicing on a sleeper sofa that was way older than I was. And that old, broken-down sofa just got better and better looking with every incarnation. My mom sewed clothes and crafted hats for herself and four kids, and our holiday family portraits hold wonderful memories of her love and creativity. My dad made furniture and loved to devise clever, homemade (yet stylish) solutions to problems, like the white-washed wooden dowel to replace the broken handle on my Mary Poppins lunch box, or the book-and-ring holder he installed over the kitchen sink so that my mom could study for her two master's degrees while washing dishes. (The fact that my mom accomplished all that while raising a family makes me a little dizzy, very grateful, and in awe of the multitasking abilities of moms everywhere!)

What I learned early on was the importance of self-reliance and creativity. That is a powerful, double-barreled lesson to learn as a child, one that has served me well and carried me through this roller coaster of life. Especially when unsure and faced with new challenges, I discovered that when I trusted my instincts and focused on the task at hand, I could usually figure it out. Don't get me wrong—I made mistakes—but I kept going. Most of us spend so much time trying to avoid mistakes that we never learn that making them is part of the process and essential to discovery.

You're about to make some discoveries yourself, with the help of Annabel! Your room (or your side of the room, if you share) is yours. It's where you go when you want to be alone, or when you need a breather or just some time to think things through. This book will help you think about how you want this space to look. It's a book of ideas—but these are just a starting point for your own individual style. Try them out, change them, and maybe come up with your own! You're going to have so much fun discovering who you are, what you like, and what makes you happy. You will be creating your own unique world: one that calms you down, fires you up, makes you laugh, makes you feel free—you decide; it's your room! The great thing about life is that the joy of creating and self-expression belongs to everyone.

I think *you* are very fortunate, too!

—Denyse

Welcome!

Hello there,

I am so glad you picked up this book! I promise it is jam-packed with awesome ideas to take your room from ho-hum to jump-up-and-down-throwing-glitter awesome. The best part is that all the awesomeness will be made by you!

(Happy dance!)

You have probably been thinking that your room needs a bit of an update, an injection of your own personal style. Hey, you are growing up! Who wants a room that cannot keep up with you and your awesome crafty style?

Hopefully you have been practicing your sewing skills. Maybe you have already tried the patterns from my first book and are feeling confident with what you can achieve with your machine.

Well, guess what—you are ready to start tackling some bigger projects. Drapes will no longer be daunting, and patchwork … not so petrifying!

I promise you can do it!

Sending crafty vibes your way,

—Annabel xo

How to Use This Book

In this book, some of the projects are pretty easy, and some are a bit more challenging. You'll notice that each project has a symbol at the top. Here's what each symbol means.

easy peasy

EASY PEASY

Start with these projects, especially if you are not super comfy yet with using your sewing machine. These are fun projects that need a little or no hand sewing. You'll have no trouble finishing these.

teeny bit challenging

A TEENY BIT MORE CHALLENGING

You'll need a little confidence for these projects. You should be comfortable using the sewing machine and with hand sewing. You are going to have so much fun with these!

take your time, ask for help

TAKE YOUR TIME AND ASK FOR HELP

These projects need some patience and a great attitude. If you really know your way around your sewing machine, go for it! I know you can do it. You may want to ask for help from an adult or other experienced sewist. We all need a little help sometimes!

tip

Practicing your skills on the easier projects in the book will help you gain confidence to tackle the more challenging ones!

I used to think that my little girl would remain my little girl well into her teens and that her floral, pink, frilly bedroom would remain her girly haven for years to come. My daughter has certainly proved me wrong.

Slowly and steadily, soft toys have made their way into clear storage bins in the basement; in their place are throw pillows that she has painted or quilted. The childlike artwork has been replaced with artfully arranged creations made with masking tape and spray paint. The pretty pink rug is gone; now bold black-and-white stripes are the "look." A little

part of my heart aches as my little girl grows into a gorgeously creative young woman. So, for these reasons, I really feel it is my job to encourage her to be the most creative person she can be.

I strongly believe that "tweens" (between child and teen) are emerging as a design-conscious group. The fact that my 12-year-old has a "dream room" board on Pinterest is kind of crazy, but also pretty cool.

Between the ages of 8 and 13, girls really start to develop their own sense of personal style. They want their havens to be more grown up … childish artwork to be replaced with artwork and decor that is a little more mature and that suits their emerging personalities and personal style. They are not adults yet, so they still love cute, but they certainly are not embracing the ruffles as they were in second grade.

I want girls to be able to pick up this book and feel excited to tackle simple and easy projects that will help them in their quest to find their own individuality.

The great thing about this book is that not only are all the projects fun, but they are also really doable for even the most inexperienced sewist.

There is no prouder moment for a parent than seeing the joy in their child who has just accomplished something on her own. These sewing projects are one way kids can challenge themselves to try something new and be successful.

Tweens are emerging as a design-conscious group.

sewing rule book

You are probably thinking to yourself: Rules? What rules could there possibly be in sewing? Sewing is meant to be fun! Yes, sewing is fun, but a few rules will help make it a great sewing experience.

1 It's All about You!

It might be hard to believe that "It's all about you!" is a rule, but the decisions you make in sewing, whether you are selecting fabrics or simply choosing a project, are really personal choices. Don't make something to be cool or to fit in, or because someone else told you that you should make it. Sewing is all about expressing yourself through your choices. Remember, if you are going to put in the time and patience it takes to create something, it should be something that you love and are proud of!

2 Take It Slow

I know you probably want to show off that gorgeous project as fast as possible, but think about it! If you rush your work, do you think that you will be happy with the outcome? Even I have to slow down when I sew. I have been known to make a mistake or two when I am rushing!

3 Be Creative

Don't be afraid of making some crazy bright fabric choices or taking one of the projects in this book and changing it up to suit yourself. That's what creativity is all about! This is your chance to express yourself. Imagine what a boring world we would live in if no one ever expressed their own creativity!

4 Practice Makes Awesomeness

So, you have just started sewing on a machine but you are busting to make a more complicated project from this book. Take my advice: Get in a little more practice! Make sure you are confident sewing a straight line, sewing with the edge of the presser foot on the edge of the fabric, sewing around corners, and threading your machine. Take a look at the Ready, Steady, Stitch Checklist. When you are able to answer yes to all the questions, you are ready to get started sewing. Yay!

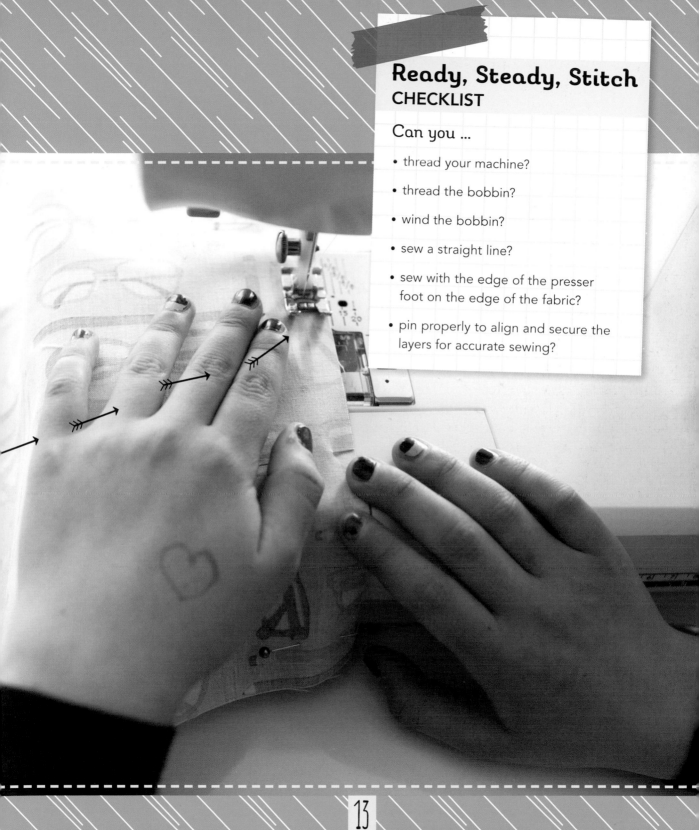

Ready, Steady, Stitch
CHECKLIST

Can you ...

- thread your machine?

- thread the bobbin?

- wind the bobbin?

- sew a straight line?

- sew with the edge of the presser foot on the edge of the fabric?

- pin properly to align and secure the layers for accurate sewing?

sewing supplies

There is nothing worse than starting a project and realizing you don't have everything you need. Let's talk about all the things you will need to get started.

 → Basic Supplies ←

All the projects have their separate supply lists; however, most of them still require you to have the basic supplies.

SEWING MACHINE AND EXTRA NEEDLES

All sewing machines are a little different. Pull out your sewing machine manual or download the manual from the Internet when you have questions about your machine. Read more about sewing machines in My Sewing Machine (page 16).

PINS

I like to use straight pearl-head pins.

SCISSORS

Make sure you have two pairs of sharp scissors. Mark one for paper and one for fabric. Cutting paper can really dull your fabric scissors!

HAND SEWING NEEDLES

Have a few hand sewing needles of different sizes on hand. You will need some with bigger eyes when you sew with embroidery floss.

SEAM RIPPER

A seam ripper is a new sewist's best friend. Always have one handy. This tool will help you rip out those "oops" stitches easily and quickly.

THREAD

Keep a variety of colors on hand.

BUTTON THREAD

Button thread is super strong and unbreakable. It is great for sewing buttons and working with heavier fabrics.

REMOVABLE-INK PEN

I love using removable-ink pens for all projects. The ink from this handy pen comes off as soon as you apply the heat from an iron. I use Pilot FriXion pens, which can be found in an office supply store.

RULER

I like to have a good 6½″ × 24″ clear ruler on hand at all times. This ruler definitely makes measuring a whole lot easier!

MEASURING TAPE

A measuring tape is so useful when you want to measure for a project that doesn't lie flat.

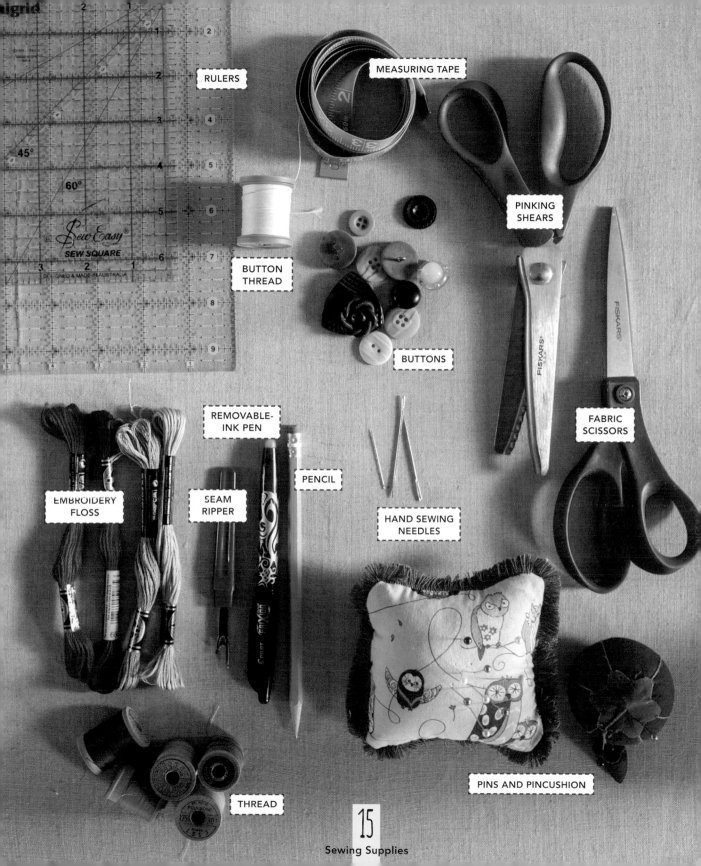

RULERS

MEASURING TAPE

PINKING SHEARS

BUTTON THREAD

BUTTONS

FABRIC SCISSORS

REMOVABLE-INK PEN

EMBROIDERY FLOSS

SEAM RIPPER

PENCIL

HAND SEWING NEEDLES

THREAD

PINS AND PINCUSHION

Sewing Supplies

My Sewing Machine

Grab your manual and take some time to familiarize yourself with your machine. I know it is hard to believe that all those buttons and knobs are important, but they are. They are also pretty fun, especially when you start experimenting with different stitches!

tip

If you need more help using your machine, you can search the Internet to find a lot of information about sewing. A book like *Me and My Sewing Machine* by Kate Haxell (C&T Publishing) is also a great resource to have and is available as an e-book that you can read on your computer or tablet.

Sewing on a sewing machine is such fun!

Threading the Machine

Most modern sewing machines have a pretty similar way of threading. It is super important to be able to thread your machine correctly. One little mistake and your machine will start sewing all higgledy-piggledy. Take a look at the sewing machine photo (page 17). Does it look a bit like your machine? Look at your manual and find a diagram on how to thread your machine; sometimes it is easier when you see a picture!

Winding the bobbin can seem a little tough at first. I promise, with a bit of practice, you will be a bobbin-winding pro! Look at the manual, ask for help, and you will be doing it in no time!

Sewing Machine Needles

Always make sure you have a full packet of sewing machine needles on hand. Some days you may break a few needles, and there is nothing worse than running out! This can happen more often when you are sewing with felt or other thick fabrics, or when you forget to take your pins out as you are sewing and hit a pin with the needle.

To change the needle, loosen the little screw beside the needle, and gently pull out the old needle. Replace the old needle with a new one, and tighten the screw super tight! (You may need to use the little screwdriver that came with your machine.)

→ The Parts of Your Machine ←

Take a closer look at the picture of the sewing machine. It should look a lot like the one you have at home. The main parts of the machine are labeled. You may be familiar with many parts already. Have a good look though; there may be some parts you are not familiar with.

If your machine has parts that are not shown in the picture, pull out your manual and find the information you are looking for. The Internet is also such a great tool. Sometimes you can find videos about your machine on YouTube. Oh, how I love the Internet!

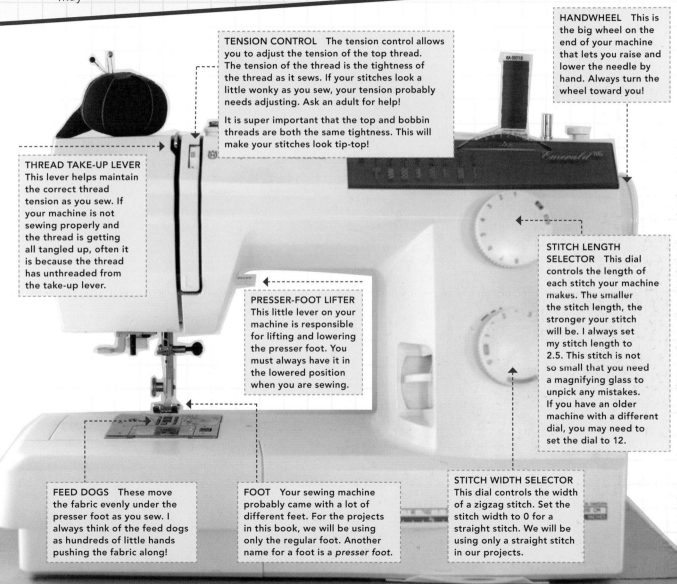

TENSION CONTROL The tension control allows you to adjust the tension of the top thread. The tension of the thread is the tightness of the thread as it sews. If your stitches look a little wonky as you sew, your tension probably needs adjusting. Ask an adult for help!

It is super important that the top and bobbin threads are both the same tightness. This will make your stitches look tip-top!

HANDWHEEL This is the big wheel on the end of your machine that lets you raise and lower the needle by hand. Always turn the wheel toward you!

THREAD TAKE-UP LEVER This lever helps maintain the correct thread tension as you sew. If your machine is not sewing properly and the thread is getting all tangled up, often it is because the thread has unthreaded from the take-up lever.

PRESSER-FOOT LIFTER This little lever on your machine is responsible for lifting and lowering the presser foot. You must always have it in the lowered position when you are sewing.

STITCH LENGTH SELECTOR This dial controls the length of each stitch your machine makes. The smaller the stitch length, the stronger your stitch will be. I always set my stitch length to 2.5. This stitch is not so small that you need a magnifying glass to unpick any mistakes. If you have an older machine with a different dial, you may need to set the dial to 12.

FEED DOGS These move the fabric evenly under the presser foot as you sew. I always think of the feed dogs as hundreds of little hands pushing the fabric along!

FOOT Your sewing machine probably came with a lot of different feet. For the projects in this book, we will be using only the regular foot. Another name for a foot is a *presser foot*.

STITCH WIDTH SELECTOR This dial controls the width of a zigzag stitch. Set the stitch width to 0 for a straight stitch. We will be using only a straight stitch in our projects.

Creating the Perfect Workspace

I know it may seem comfy, but perching your sewing machine on your bed and using your hand to work the pedal is just not the best way to start out sewing!

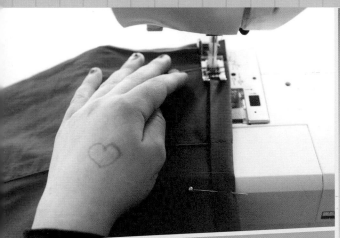

Let There Be Light

Light is really important. You will need more light for your project than the little light on your sewing machine can provide. Make sure you have good overhead lighting or a nice, bright table lamp.

Sewing Table

A sewing table can be a dining room table or a table in your room. Just make sure that it is a good flat surface and is not too tall or too low for you.

Save the Snacking for Break Time

Sadly, as careful as you try to be, if you eat a cookie in your sewing space, the crumbs will surely make their way into all the nooks and crannies of your machine. Let's not even talk about what would happen if you spilled a glass of milk. Yikes!

Sewing Chair

Although it is important to be comfy, your chair needs to be firm and supportive ... there is no slouch in sewing!

Supplies

Always make sure that your sewing supplies are handy and within reach. Storage baskets are a great way to keep everything neat as a pin! Why not make a few Mod Stamped Storage Baskets (page 87)?

Creating a fun and functional workspace may be one of the most important parts of setting the scene for successful sewing!

My absolute favorite part of starting a new project is choosing my fabrics. Your project can look completely different depending on the fabric you choose. Your ottoman can go from mod to girly; it is all in the fabric!

Find fabrics at your local quilt shop, fabric store, or thrift shop! The fabrics I mainly like to use are felt, quilting cotton, upholstery-weight cotton, and thicker cotton canvas.

Felt

I will never get tired of working with felt! It really is a wonderful fabric for all types of sewing and crafting. I prefer to work with wool felt, but that is sometimes a little tricky to find. Your local fabric and craft stores are sure to have a gazillion colors of fun eco and synthetic felt.

The great thing about felt is that when you cut the edges, it doesn't fray! That means you never really need to hem felt. This is why I love to use it when cutting out letters and unusual shapes.

did you know?
Eco felt is made from recycled plastic bottles.

Cotton

For the projects in this book, cotton is the main fabric to use. I really love using quilting cotton. It is lightweight, easy to sew, and comes in so many amazing colors and patterns that you are sure to have a hard time choosing your favorite. You should be able to find a really great selection at your local fabric store. A lot of websites also have super awesome selections to choose from.

For some of the projects that need sturdier fabric, I look for decorator-weight fabrics. They are cotton also but tend to have a little more stiffness, which is really important for pillows and other projects that need to have some weight to them.

Cotton Canvas

Cotton canvas is an awesome basic fabric that is perfect for projects that involve any kind of stamping and stenciling. It is a great stiff fabric and comes in a natural, undyed color. Just think of it as your blank artist's canvas, and let your creativity flow!

Repurposing and Recycling

Everyone knows I love thrift shopping. I am not necessarily looking for some great outfit but rather for fab fabrics and buttons. You would be surprised at how many amazing vintage clothes end up on the racks.

Don't be put off by the prospect of visiting a thrift shop; embrace it! Usually, a good wash is all the clothes need, and they are ready to be cut apart and repurposed into something truly awesome and one-of-a-kind. It's fun to look at things and see another purpose!

special skills

As you start working on the projects in this book, you will see that many of them involve some special skills. Don't be alarmed! These are just skills that you may not have tried before. Some may require you to ask for help, and some will be easy for you to do yourself. Don't you just love learning new skills?

>>> → Using a Hot Glue Gun ← ≪

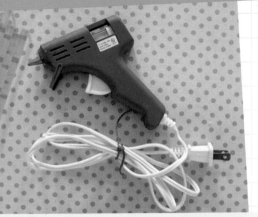

I love hot glue guns! They really are the most marvelous invention!

We will be using the hot glue gun for many of the projects in this book. The main thing to remember about using a hot glue gun is that it is *hot*! Make sure you only use a low-temperature glue gun. This tool will be hot enough to do the job, but won't give you a nasty burn if you happen to glue your fingers together!

→ Using Fusible Web >>>

I love fusible web! It is a great product to use when you want to apply one fabric to another fabric without pinning. Most fusible web has paper over a sticky webbing that acts like glue when heated with an iron. It is super handy when you are sewing down felt letters or other felt shapes. My favorites are HeatnBond Lite and Lite Steam-A-Seam. These products are easy to find at your local fabric or craft store.

1.

Turn the steam setting off on your iron.

2.

Trace the shape you need onto the paper side of the fusible web.

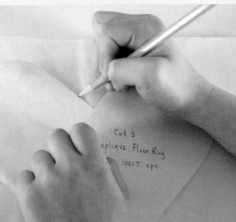

If you are working with letters, make sure to trace them backward.

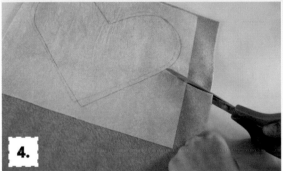

TIP Always read the manufacturer's directions before using fusible web. They may give you different tips on working with their products.

3.

Leave the paper on, and place the sticky side down onto the back of the fabric. Iron for a few seconds to fuse in place.

4.

After the fabric has cooled down, cut out the shape.

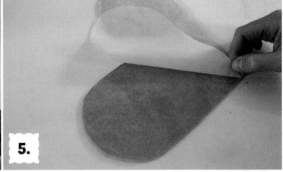

5.

Peel off the backing paper.

6. & 7.

Position the shape or letters on your fabric with the sticky side down.

Iron the shape until it is super tight!

Now you are ready to sew around the outside of the shape!

Sewing a Button

I love buttons and have been collecting them for years. Whenever I am at my local thrift store, I keep my eyes peeled for some fun ones. I have even been known to buy a piece of clothing from a thrift shop just because I loved the buttons! Adding a button or two to a sewing project can really make your project pop!

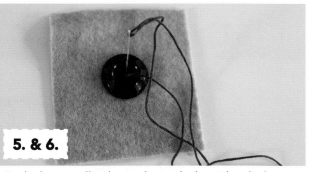

Sewing on a button is really easy. Once you have mastered it, it's a piece of cake!

1. Use the removable-ink pen or a pin to mark the spot for your button.

2. Thread your needle with button thread.

3. Tie a double knot in the end of the thread. Be sure to leave a long tail of thread past the knot.

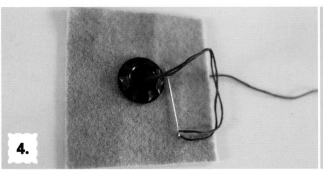

4.

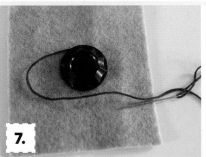

5. & 6.

Put the button on the fabric. Hold it down with your thumb. Bring the needle up from underneath the fabric. Poke it through one of the buttonholes. Pull it all the way through.

Push the needle down through the other hole and out through the back of the fabric.

Repeat Steps 4 and 5. Do them 2 or 3 times until the button feels nice and secure.

7.

Bring the needle up from underneath the fabric, but don't put the needle through the hole. Instead, wrap it around underneath the button a few times.

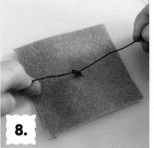

8.

Bring the needle back down to the underside of the fabric. Tie a knot with the starter thread tail. Trim your threads, and you are done!

»»»→ Using Patterns ←«««

A few projects have pattern pieces in the back of the book for you to use. All the pattern pieces are just the right size for you to trace and use. I like to trace my pattern pieces on parchment paper. Parchment paper is a white, translucent paper that comes on a roll. It makes a really great tracing paper because you can easily see through it and you can easily find it in the baking aisle of the supermarket.

> You can easily find parchment paper in the baking aisle of the supermarket.

How to Use a Pattern

1. Lay the parchment paper over the pattern. Use a pencil to trace the pattern lines neatly onto the paper. Parchment paper is translucent enough that you should have no problem seeing the lines.

TIP Some pattern pieces need to be joined together when traced to make one parchment paper pattern. Follow the project directions; it is easy to do.

2. Using paper scissors, cut out the shape on the lines.

3. Lay the paper pattern piece on your fabric, pin it in place, and trace around it. (If you are good at cutting, you can skip the tracing and just cut around the pinned pattern.) Remove the pattern.

4. Using fabric scissors, carefully cut around the traced line.

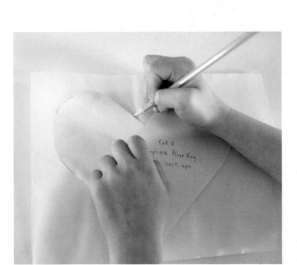

Using a Staple Gun

Have you ever used a staple gun before? I am sure you have seen an adult using one. Well, great news! With a bit of help and supervision, you can be using a staple gun like a pro!

What You Need to Know

- Always ask an adult for help.

- Make sure you are using the correct staples to fit your gun. There are many different sizes to choose from. (Your box will tell you what size staples you need.)

- Never use a staple gun unless it is facedown. Some power guns have a safety mechanism that will stop the gun from working unless it is pressed down on a surface.

- Use firm pressure when using a staple gun. If you have trouble with this, ask a grown-up for help.

TIP Never use a staple gun without adult supervision. They are awesome tools but can be dangerous if not used correctly.

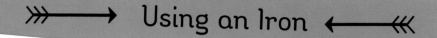

Using an Iron

It is important to learn how to use an iron correctly. An iron is an essential tool for creating a beautiful-looking project.

Here Are a Few Tips:

- Keep your fingers away from the hot iron when you are using it on the fabric.

- Pay attention to the type of fabric you are ironing. Cotton can take high heat, but some fabrics cannot hold up to high heat. The last thing you want is a piece of melted fabric on your hands. Make sure the dial of your iron is set to the correct fabric setting, such as cotton or wool.

- Never leave the iron with the soleplate down on your fabric.

- Always turn off your iron when you are finished.

Hand Sewing

I know you love sewing on the sewing machine, but did you know that hand sewing is just as important? Hand sewing can take a little time to master, but once you do, there is no looking back. Imagine all the beautiful things you can stitch after you have the hang of it!

Running Stitch

The running stitch is the most basic and simple of all hand sewing stitches. It is basically just an up-and-down stitch.

1. Knot your thread at the end. Poke the needle up from underneath the fabric, and pull the thread through to the top.

2. Next, poke the needle back down ¼˝ away. Pull the thread through to the back of the fabric again. Repeat this all along the seam. Keep your stitches even and neat.

tip

Sometimes it helps to draw little dots on your fabric with a removable-ink pen. Draw them equal distances apart, and use them as a stitching guide. Simply apply the heat of the iron when you are finished, and the pen marks will disappear!

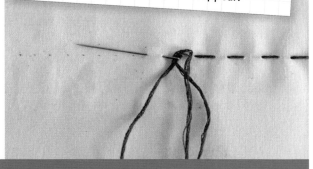

Whipstitch

Whipstitch is used for closing up openings in things like pillows and softies.

1. Tie a knot in the end of your thread.

2. Bring the needle up from behind the fabric.

Bring the needle over the edge of the fabric to the back, and bring it up through the fabric again just a little to one side of the last stitch.

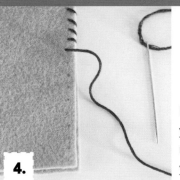

4.

Keep doing this until you are finished. Try really hard to keep your stitches neat and even.

5. Don't forget to tie a knot when you get to the end.

Blanket Stitch

I do love the look of the blanket stitch. It gives a project that sweet, handmade look. And of course, once you get the hang of it, you will love doing it too!

1. Cut a nice long piece of embroidery floss. Be sure to tie a knot in the end.

2.

Bring the needle up from behind the fabric.

3.

Push the needle down through the fabric beside the last stitch. Don't pull it all the way through; you want it to make a little loop. Bring the needle through the loop, and pull firmly.

4. Keep doing this all the way around the edge of your project until you get back to where you started.

5.

When you get to the end, instead of bringing the needle through the back again, thread it through the first angled stitch you made at the beginning. Bring the needle to the back of the fabric, sewing 2 or 3 little stitches to hold everything in place.

sewing terms

These projects may have some words that have you scratching your head and thinking, "What does that mean?" Here are your questions answered!

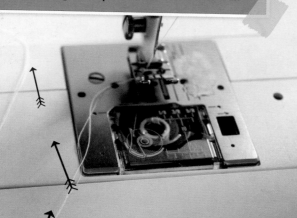

Leave a Tail

I really hate when my machine comes unthreaded. I have an easy tip so that does not happen to you. Pull out an 8″-long "tail" of machine and bobbin thread before you begin sewing. That way, when the machine needle goes down, it won't take your thread with it.

Backstitch

It is important to backstitch at the beginning and end of every stitch line. Backstitching just creates a strong anchoring stitch that prevents your stitching from coming undone. Most machines have a reverse button that you will need to hold down to go backward. Take a look at your machine manual to find it.

When you start sewing a seam, sew a few stitches forward, and then hold down the reverse button for a few stitches. Now let go of the button and continue forward until the end of the seam. When you get to the end of the seam, hold down the reverse button again to secure the stitches.

Edge of the Presser Foot on the Edge of the Fabric

The projects in this book are sewn using the regular presser foot that comes with most sewing machines. For that reason, these projects use a ⅜″ seam allowance. That means that most of the projects can simply be sewn with the edge of the foot on the edge of the fabric!

This sure is a funny name; I am sure you are thinking, "What is a fat quarter?"

Fat Quarter

A fat quarter is a quarter of a yard of fabric, but it is not a regular quarter yard, which is 9″ × 44″; it has a different shape. To get a fat quarter of fabric, you would divide one yard of quilting fabric into four large rectangles, so each rectangle measures 18″ × 22″.

Fat quarters are great because you can actually get more usable fabric out of this measurement than with a regular quarter yard.

Right Sides Together

It is important to sew with right sides together. To do this, match up the fabrics with the pretty (right) sides facing each other. This means that you will be sewing with the wrong side of the fabric facing you. This way, when you turn your project right side out, no messy raw edges will be showing.

Wrong side

Right side

No-Sew Zone

You will come across the term *no-sew zone* in this book. This is my own made-up term for the area where you don't sew … you know, when you are sewing a piece that needs to be turned right side out.

Seam

Seam

This is the line you have sewn to join one piece of fabric to another piece of fabric.

Seam Allowance

This is the measurement from the edge of the fabric to the stitching line. The seam allowance for most of the projects in this book is ⅜˝. If your presser foot measures only ¼˝, you could use a piece of painter's tape as a guide and sew with the edge of the fabric on the edge of the painter's tape. I think it really helps when you have some way to line everything up!

Seam allowance

Sewing Around a Corner

For some projects in this book, you will need to sew around the sides of a square or a rectangle. This means that you will also have to sew around a corner.

Start at the top right side, and beginning with a backstitch, stitch down to the bottom corner. Stop the machine, make sure the needle is down in the fabric, lift the presser foot, and turn your fabric. Lower the presser foot, and sew to the next corner. Continue doing this until you have sewn all four sides.

Don't forget to backstitch at the end.

Topstitch

Top stitch

Sew a straight stitch to give your work a neat, finished look. It is usually a line sewn between ⅛˝ and ¼˝ from the edge around the outside of a completed project.

If you feel worried about creating a neat stitch, you can draw the line with a removable-ink pen first and then sew on that line.

finding your inspiration

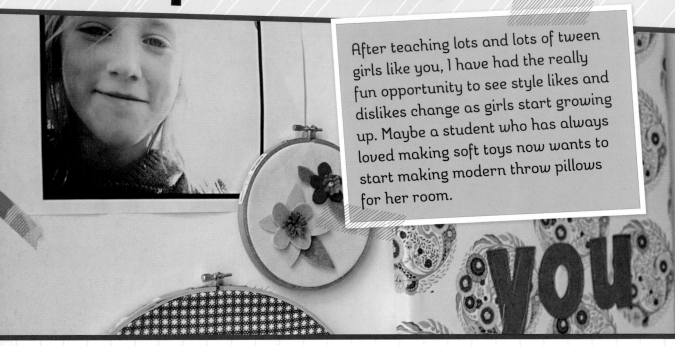

After teaching lots and lots of tween girls like you, I have had the really fun opportunity to see style likes and dislikes change as girls start growing up. Maybe a student who has always loved making soft toys now wants to start making modern throw pillows for her room.

This is a time in your life when you are probably spending a lot more time in your bedroom doing homework. You want to create a space for yourself that expresses your individuality and sense of style while also showing how crafty you are.

You know you love bold colors and modern shapes, but you also love fun flowers and cute animal prints. You still love pink, but maybe not for the walls.

Maybe you want to start packing away some of your artwork. You are feeling like you want to start expressing your personality through a new, more grown-up look.

I am sure you have looked through magazines or seen something on TV that makes you think, "I would love my room to look like that!"

The hardest part is that moment when you realize that you love all these things but really have no idea where to start.

This is the point when you need to find your inspiration!

Mood Boards

A mood board is a place to store all your inspiration, whether it is a picture you tore out of a magazine or a small, beautifully colored bead. A mood board is an amazing tool that allows you to gather all your inspiration in one place!

Whenever I am working on a project, I like to use a wall in my office where I can tape pieces of fabric, torn-out pages, photos, and other bits and bobs as inspiration for color and design. It is a really fun thing to do and is a great idea for you to try when you start thinking about updating your space!

⟫—→ Make One

You could use a cork memo board, a piece of cardboard, or even a wall to create your mood board.

tip

If you are using a wall, masking tape works really well to attach your images. The best thing is, it won't damage the wall, and that will surely make your parents happy!

Start with a photo or scrap of fabric as your main dream piece. For me, I always start with a color. So let's say that you love turquoise and you would like that in your room. Make that color the first thing you pin or tape on the board.

Now start to add other things you like: a patchwork skirt that would look awesome as a headboard, a chandelier that makes you feel happy, a scrap of fabric from the craft store.

Keep layering and layering ideas until you have a board in front of you that tells the story of your own style.

When you are happy with what you have created, **use this as a jumping-off point** to search out pieces and fabrics that work with the feel you want to create. It doesn't have to cost much; in fact, sometimes handmade items and a lick of paint will totally transform a space.

Mod ← «

Whimsical » →

Boho ←———≪

Patchy ≫———→

Pinterest

I am pretty sure you know how to use the computer, right? If you feel confident with the computer and, of course, have your parent's permission, you could check out this website called Pinterest.

Pinterest is a great online pin board. You can look through photos of anything from cool rooms to cute puppies, and whenever you see something that you like, you can "pin" it to your own board. You can create a lot of boards for all your different interests.

You might even want to set up a Pinterest board with the title "my room."

TIP

Remember to ask your parents for permission before you sign in to any new website!

Collecting Inspiration

You can collect inspiration wherever you go.

Have you ever picked up a fall leaf and looked, I mean, *really* looked, at the shape, color, and lines on that leaf? The veins may inspire you to create artwork for your room. The leaf color may steer you in a color direction for the paint, and the shape of the leaf may inspire you to make a garland of leaves from felt. Whoa! Who knew a leaf could be so darn inspiring?

Go out into the world and look around you. Go to the public library and look at magazines; print pictures from the Internet; visit thrift shops and delve into the bric-a-brac boxes for do-it-yourself ideas and inspiration.

Your inspiration is out there; you just need to get out there and find it!

Maybe it is a color that inspires you.
Use your newly found mood board skills
to create a mini color mood board.

39

Thrifting for Great Fabrics

So, you have chosen a color and a look, and you are ready to start looking for fabric to make one of these fun projects. You can go to craft and fabric stores to find what you need, or you can visit your local thrift shop for inspiration.

Check out the racks of clothing in your local thrift store. The fabric in a kooky pair of pants may be just what you need for a patchwork project, and that moth-eaten sweater may work beautifully for your chandelier project.

You never know—there may even be an old set of drapes just calling your name to be refashioned into a throw!

Remember, thrift shops require a bit of digging, but they are always very cheap, and you can usually find something cool at them that you normally would not have looked at before!

tip
Be sure to wash your thrift shop fabric purchases before sewing your masterpiece.

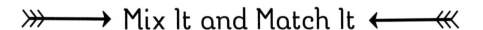
⫸⟶ Mix It and Match It ⟵⫷

Those Mod Stamped Storage Baskets could be pretty awesome if they were patchy. That lampshade could look super cool if it was stamped with a modern design. How about some whimsically inspired drapes? Using the same basic principles of construction, you can start to think creatively and outside the box to reimagine some of these projects. We all want to be creative, right?

The great thing about decorating a space is that it is your space, and the only rules that need apply are your own.

You should never be afraid to mix things up to suit your style.

So often we are told that this should match that and that you should never mix this pattern with that pattern. Here is your chance to experiment a little. All the projects in this book fit in a kind of theme, but I tried hard not to make anything too matchy-matchy. So go ahead, mix and match away! All I ask is that you have fun with it!

Happy sewing!

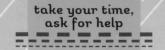

SCRAPPY STRIP
Memo Board

Finished size: 23″ × 17″

What Do I Need?

- Strips of fabric in all different widths (Each strip should measure at least 24″ long.)

- Felt scrap for pocket measuring at least 6″ × 6″

- Batting measuring at least 26″ × 20″

- Pinking shears

- 1 wood-framed cork memo board measuring 23″ × 17″

- Staple gun

- 2 eye screws

- 1 piece of ribbon or twine

- Basic Supplies (page 14)

TIP You can find cork memo boards at most craft and office supply stores. (The sizes may vary a little from what I used.)

SPECIAL SKILLS

- Using a Staple Gun (page 26) • Using an Iron (page 27)
- Sewing Terms (page 30)

Prepare the Pieces

1. Cut a variety of fabric strips in different widths. I cut strips from 1½″ to 4″ wide.

2. Line up your fabric strips in the order that you want to sew them. (It is great to get a visual look at how the fabrics work together before you start sewing.) Cut enough strips to add up to at least 30″ across.

3. Cut a piece of felt 6″ × 6″ for the pocket.

4. Cut a piece of batting 26″ × 20″.

5. Use a pair of pinking shears to give all 4 sides of the pocket a decorative edge.

6. Sew a neat top stitch across the top of the pocket.

Wouldn't you love to have a place to show off all your special things? Sports ribbons, artwork, love letters? This fun and scrappy memo board will be the perfect place to keep all your mementos in one place. Choose a fun color scheme that works well with your room.

Scrappy Strip Memo Board

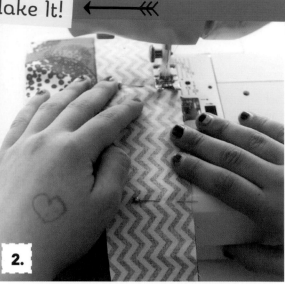

1.

Take your first and second strips, and lay them right sides together, matching the long sides. Pin them in place.

2.

Sew the pieces together, with the edge of the presser foot on the edge of the fabric.

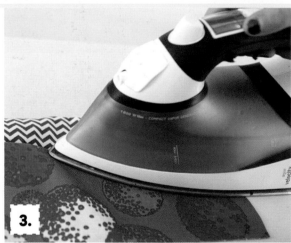

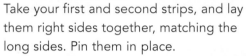

3.

Iron the strips open.

4.

Attach a third strip in the same way, pin, and sew.

5. & 6.

Iron the strips open.

Continue sewing the strips until the scrappy strip panel measures at least 28″ wide. Add more strips if you need to.

7.

Trim the ironed panel down to 28″ × 22″.

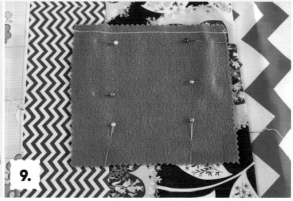

8.

Lay the panel on top of the corkboard to work out the pocket placement.

9.

Position the pocket, and pin it in place.

10.

Sew the pocket in place. Make sure to sew nice and close to the edge, and be sure to leave the top of the pocket open.

1. Lay the scrappy patch panel right side down on a sturdy flat table.

2. Lay the piece of batting centered on top.

(You may need to ask for help here.)

3. Lay the corkboard on the top of the fabric and batting stack. Make sure it is centered.

4. & 5. Start by pulling the fabric taut and wrapping it around the edges of the board.

Staple in the center of each side edge to hold the fabric in place.

6. Add a couple more staples to both sides of that first staple.

7. Carefully bring the fabric up over the edges of the wooden frame, starting with the corners. Fold in the edges neatly.

8. & 9.

Staple in place.

Continue to staple all the way around, until the board and fabric are super secure!

10.

Screw in a pair of eye screws on each side, making sure each screw is the same distance from the top of the frame. String on a piece of ribbon or twine, and you are done!

Now hang your gorgeous memo board, and admire your handiwork!

Simple Patch Throw

Finished size: 43¾″ × 52½″

What Do I Need?

- 30 fabric squares, measuring 9½″ × 9½″

- Cotton quilt batting, measuring at least 45″ × 54″

- 1½-yard piece of fabric for the backing

- Removable-ink pen

- Yarn

- Embroidery needle

- Basic Supplies (page 14)

SPECIAL SKILLS

- Using an Iron (page 27)
- Sewing Terms (page 30)

Prepare the Pieces

1. Cut 30 fabric squares, from all different fabrics, each measuring 9½″ × 9½″.

TIP I usually like to cut my squares from a variety of print fabrics, approximately 5 squares from each print.

2. Cut the batting to measure 45″ × 54″.

3. Cut the backing fabric to measure 45″ × 54″.

Let's Make It!

1.

Lay out your 9½″ fabric squares so that the design is positioned the way you want it, with 5 squares across and 6 squares down.

There is nothing better on a chilly night than to snuggle up in a cozy quilt. This quilt will not only be cozy but also be made by you! How cool is that?

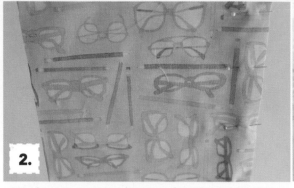

2.

Working in rows, take your first 2 squares, lay them right sides together, and pin one side.

3.

Sew with the edge of the presser foot on the edge of the fabric.

4.

Iron the squares open.

5. & 6.

tip

I like to pin a little piece of paper to the first square of each row. I number each piece of paper so that I don't forget which row goes where.

Repeat Steps 2–4 until an entire row of 5 squares is sewn together and ironed.

Do the same thing with all your squares so that you end up with a total of 6 patch rows.

7.

Take your first and second rows, and lay them right sides together, being sure to match the seams. Pin in place.

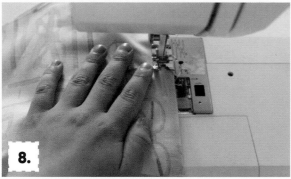

8.

9.

Sew the long edge of the 2 rows together, with the edge of the presser foot on the edge of the fabric.

Iron the rows open.

10. Continue doing this until all the rows are sewn together.

11. Give it one final iron, and you are done with this part!

Let's Put It All Together!

1. Lay the batting on a large flat surface.

2. Lay the patchwork top right side up on top of the batting. Using the patchwork top as the guide, cut around the batting to make it the same size. Set the batting aside.

3. Lay the backing right side up and lay the patchwork top right side down on the backing. Using the top as a guide, cut the backing to the correct size.

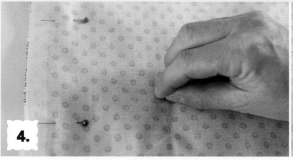

4.

5.

Now lay the layered backing and patchwork top on top of the batting from Step 3. Make sure the edges are even, and pin all the way around.

Mark a 4″ line on one side of the throw. This will be our no-sew zone. We will need this hole to turn the throw right side out!

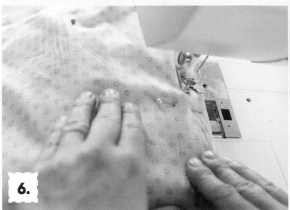

6.

With the edge of the presser foot on the edge of the fabric, sew all the way around the 4 sides of the throw. *Remember:* Don't sew in the no-sew zone!

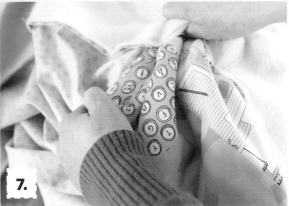

7.

Reach between the 2 layers of fabric, and pull the throw right side out through the hole. Make sure the batting remains in the center.

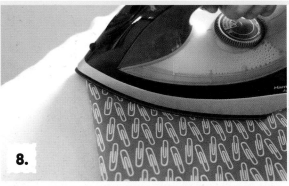

8.

Push out all the corners, and give it a really good iron.

9.

Turn the raw edges of the hole to the inside. Pin the hole closed.

10. Sew up the hole with the sewing machine. Sew nice and close to the edge.

11. Use the iron to remove the ink.

Tying a throw is a great way to hold all the layers together, and it also looks super cute!

1. Cut an arm's length of fun yarn and thread it onto a sharp embroidery needle.

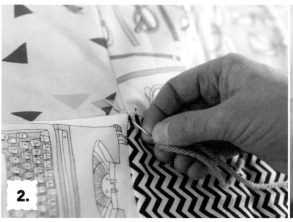

At a patchwork square corner, bring the needle down through all the layers and then up again right beside where you started.

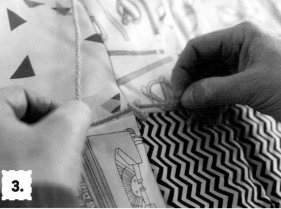

Tie a double knot in your yarn.

Cut off the yarn ends to approximately ½″–1″.

Tie a knot in the corner of each of the patchwork squares. Keep going until you are done.

Hooray! Doesn't your throw look amazing?

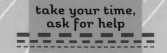
LARGE PATCH
Headboard

Finished size: 30″ × 40″

What Do I Need?

- 20 fabric squares, measuring 10½″ × 10½″
- 12 self-covering buttons, size 2″
- Small scraps of fabric for the self-covering buttons
- 2 pieces of low-loft batting, measuring 32″ × 42″
- Stretched artist canvas, measuring 30″ × 40″
- Staple gun
- Button thread
- Basic Supplies (page 14)

SPECIAL SKILLS

- Sewing a Button (page 24)
- Using a Staple Gun (page 26)
- Using an Iron (page 27)
- Sewing Terms (page 30)

Prepare the Pieces

1. Cut 20 squares from different fabrics, each measuring 10½″ × 10½″.

(For this project, I like using at least 2 of each print.)

2. Following the instructions on the packet, make 12 size 2″ covered buttons.

Let's Make It!

The Patchwork

1.

Lay out your fabric squares with 5 squares across and 4 squares down.

What better place to lay your head than against your very own, super custom patch headboard! Your friends will be asking where on earth you got it, and you can proudly tell them, "I made it!"

2. Working in rows, take your first 2 squares, lay them right sides together, and pin.

3. Sew the 2 squares together, with the edge of the presser foot on the edge of the fabric.

4. Iron the squares open.

5. Repeat these steps until the entire row of 5 squares is sewn together and ironed.

6. Do this with all your rows so that you end up with 4 patch rows.

7. Take your first and second rows, and lay them right sides together, being sure to match the seams. Pin in place.

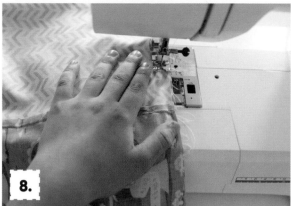

8.

9.

Sew the long edge of the 2 rows together, with the edge of the foot on the edge of the fabric.

Iron the rows open.

10. Continue doing this until all the rows are sewn together.

11. Give it one final iron, and you are done with the patchwork panel!

Let's Put It All Together!

1. Lay your patchwork panel right side down on a large flat surface.

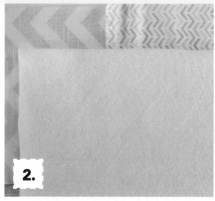

2.

3.

TIP
You may want to use a ruler to measure around the fabric edges. Make sure that the canvas is perfectly centered on the patchy panel.

Center the 2 pieces of batting on top of the patchwork panel.

Lay the stretched artist canvas right side down in the center of the patchwork and batting stack.

4. & 5.

Start by wrapping the fabric and batting tightly around the edges of the canvas.

With help from an adult, use the staple gun to put an anchoring staple in the center of each side edge of the frame. Staple through the fabric, batting, and frame to hold the layers in place.

Time to tackle the corners.

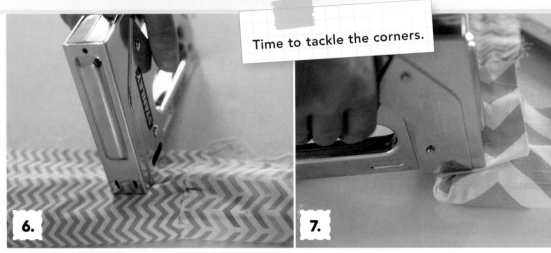

6.

7.

Staple on each side of those initial anchoring staples.

First, pull the fabric over the corner, and anchor it with a staple.

Then, gently fold the fabric in on either side of that point, and staple into place.

8. Continue stapling around the rest of the canvas until everything is nice and secure.

1.

Using a sharp needle threaded with button thread, push the needle from behind through the canvas at the point where the patch squares intersect.

2.

Push the needle through the loop underneath the covered button.

3.

Push the needle back down through to the back of the canvas.

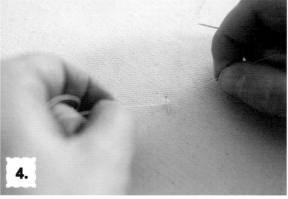

4.

Tie a tight triple knot, and trim the threads.

5.

Continue to do this, sewing all your buttons to the headboard.

All done! You can easily hang this lightweight headboard on a couple of nails in the wall!

How awesome and professional does your headboard look?

Simple Window Panel

Finished size: 49″ wide × the length you decide on

What Do I Need?

- 5 squares of quilting fabric measuring 10½″ × 10½″
- Twin-size flat bed sheet
- Basic Supplies (page 14)

SPECIAL SKILLS

- Using an Iron (page 27)
- Sewing Terms (page 30)

Prepare the Pieces

1. For each separate curtain panel, you will need a twin flat sheet and 5 squares cut to measure 10½″ × 10½″.

2. With an adult's help, measure from your curtain rod to the floor or windowsill.

Add 5½″ to your measurement. This will be the length you need to cut the sheet.

3. Cut the sheet so it measures 51″ wide.

TIP Remove the hemmed edges when you cut the sheet to size.

tip Many windows need more than one curtain panel to cover them. Measure the width of your window; if it is more than 36″ wide, you will need to make 2 curtain panels per window.

Let's Make It!

The Sheet

Iron the sheet, fold in the long sides of the sheet ½″ toward the wrong side, fold over again ½″ toward the wrong side, and iron again.

1.

2. & 3.

Secure the fold with some pins.

Do this with both long sides.

Don't be daunted by the prospect of sewing drapes. With this easy project, you will be making them for the whole house!

Simple Window Panel

tip

Use a thread color to match your fabric color.

4.

5. Do the same thing with the bottom of the sheet. You will hem the top edge later.

Sew nice and close to each folded-in edge.

The Patchwork

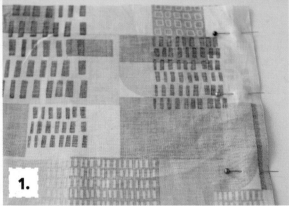

1.

Take 2 of your different fabric squares, and pin them right sides together along one side.

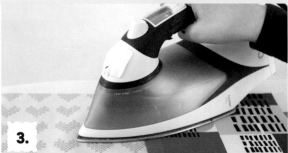

2.

Sew them together, with the edge of the presser foot on the edge of the fabric.

3.

Iron the 2 squares open.

4.

Continue attaching pieces together until you have a row of 5 squares.

5.

6.

Fold in the long sides of the patchy strip ¼″, and iron in place. Do this to both long sides.

Fold under the short edges ¼″, and iron in place.

You may find that your patchy strip comes out a bit longer than the width of the sheet. Don't worry! Just fold in and iron the short edges to the perfect width!

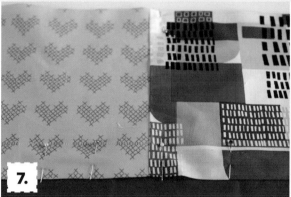

7.

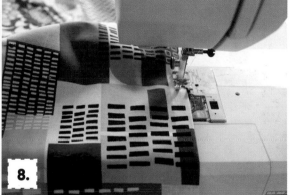

8.

Lay the patchy strip along the bottom hemmed edge of the sheet panel, and pin in place, making sure to line the edges up perfectly.

Sew the strip in place by stitching close to the edge, down both long sides of the strip.

9. Sew the short ends nice and close to the edge.

Repeat all these steps to create more curtain panels.

Finish Up

1. Fold over the top of the panel ½″, and iron in place.

2. Fold over again 4″, and iron.

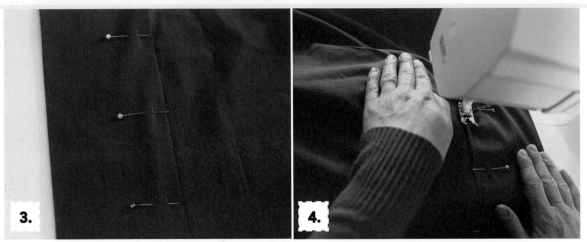

3. Pin in place.

4. Sew nice and close to the folded edge.

5. Trim all the loose threads.

With a little help from an adult, slide a curtain rod through the top of your panel, and you're all done! Time to hang your glorious panels. Don't they look fantastic?

Plush Geometric Mobile

What Do I Need?

- Felt scraps
- Parchment paper
- Removable-ink pen
- Fun-colored thread
- Polyfill stuffing
- Fishing line
- Branch or piece of wood
- Twine

SPECIAL SKILLS

- Using Patterns (page 25)
- Using an Iron (page 27)

Prepare the Pieces

1. Trace the gem pattern (page 166) onto parchment paper.

2. Cut 14 gems out of felt (make 2 of each color), to make 7 matching pairs.

3. Using the removable-ink pen, draw the gem details on the felt pieces. Look at the pattern piece for guidance.

Let's Make It!

>>> ➤ **Let's Make It!** ← ≪

1.

Thread your machine with a fun color. Stitch along all the gem lines. After stitching, you can iron the gems to remove the ink!

Who says diamonds are only for wearing on your fingers? This fun mobile brings in some neon bling and brightens up even the dreariest corner of your room!

Plush Geometric Mobile

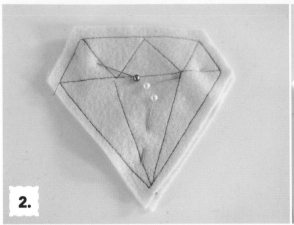

2.

With wrong sides together, place 2 gem pieces together, and pin in place.

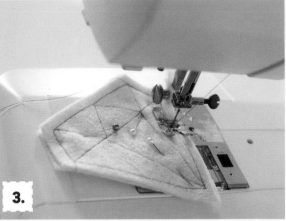

3.

Sew around the outer edge of the gems on top of the edge stitching. Leave a little opening along one side for stuffing.

4.

Stuff the gem with a little stuffing. You don't want it to be too fat; just a little will do.

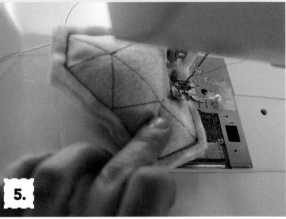

5.

Sew the open edge closed.

6. & 7.

8.

Repeat Steps 2–5 to make 7 gems.

Thread a needle with fishing line. Sew once through the top and center of the gem.

Tie the fishing line in a knot on top of the gem.

9.

10. & 11.

Think about other shapes that would look good on a mobile. Bird shapes would also be cute!

Decide on the length to hang the gem, and tie the other end of the fishing line on your piece of wood.

Do this with the other gems, making sure to space them evenly across the length of the wood and hang them at all different lengths.

Tie a fun-colored piece of twine to each end of the branch, and hang your fun, mod mobile for all to enjoy!

Pillows:
Three Ways

Finished size: 19¼″ × 19¼″

⟩⟩⟩→ Paint Splatter Pillow

Who said that splattered paint = mess?
These splattered pillows are the perfect
artwork for your room.

What Do I Need?

- ¾ yard of natural canvas fabric,
  at least 54″ wide

- Drop cloth

- 1 small bottle of fabric paint

- Plastic disposable bowl

- Spoon

- Iron

- Old towel

- Clothes you can get messy

SPECIAL SKILLS

- Using an Iron (page 27)

For this project, we will be using one simple pillow pattern and working on three different decorative techniques to create our own fabric! The great thing about it—they all look fab piled high on your bed!

71

Let's Make It!

We need to start by cutting our front pillow panel.

1. Cut a 20″ × 20″ square of canvas fabric.

2. Lay your drop cloth down somewhere outside.

3. & 4.

5.

Lay the canvas fabric on top of the drop cloth.

Pour paint into a little bowl.

Splatter paint onto the canvas fabric using the spoon to flick the paint. Be sure you're wearing clothes that can get messy.

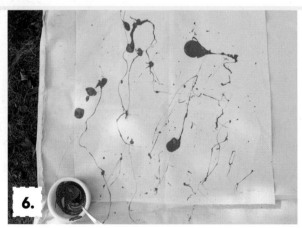
6.

When you are happy with your work, leave the canvas to dry overnight.

7. When the canvas is totally dry, you can lay an old towel over the painted area, and run an iron over it. This will set the paint.

8. Skip to Time to Make the Pillows! (page 79) to finish your pillow.

→ Bleached-Out Heart Pillow

So bleach conjures up images of scrubbing the floor? Let's look at its powers in another way by creating an awesome bleached heart effect on denim.

What Do I Need?

- ¾ yard of dark denim fabric, at least 54˝ wide

- Drop cloth

- Removable-ink pen

- Plastic disposable bowl

- Small cup of bleach

- Old paintbrush

- Washing machine

- Apron or old clothes

- Iron

SPECIAL SKILLS

- Using an Iron (page 27)

>>> → Let's Make It! ← «<

We need to start by cutting our front pillow panel.

1. Cut a 20″ × 20″ square of denim fabric.

2. In an open, well-ventilated area, lay down a drop cloth to protect your work area.

3. Place your denim fabric with the right side facing up.

tip

You can use the heart-shape pattern (page 166) to create a parchment paper pattern (see Using Patterns, page 25) or draw the heart freehand.

Draw a heart shape using your removable-ink pen. (It looks best if it is centered on the square.)

TIP

Bleach is a dangerous chemical, so you should use caution and ask for help when using it. Always make sure you use bleach outside or in a well-ventilated room. Also, make sure you wear an apron or some old clothes when you are using bleach; it can really damage your clothes if it splashes on them. If you happen to get bleach on your hands, be sure to wash them well right away. It's always a good idea to read the caution note on the bleach bottle.

Pour bleach into the plastic bowl. Make sure you are wearing an apron and working in a well-ventilated area because bleach has harmful fumes.

6.

Dip your paintbrush into the bleach, and starting at the outside edge, evenly paint your heart with the bleach.

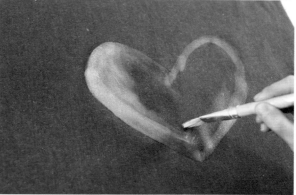

You should paint over the area a couple of times.

7.

Leave the fabric for 30 minutes; the heart should have become very pale and bleached out.

> **tip**
>
> Don't leave bleach on the denim for more than 30 minutes. The bleach can eat through the fabric, and instead of a heart, you will find a hole!

8. Throw your piece of fabric in the washing machine and ask an adult to turn on the cold cycle. After the wash, throw it in the dryer.

9. Give it a good iron.

Skip to Time to Make the Pillows! (page 79); now you're ready to finish the pillow!

→ Painted Chevron Pillow

Masking tape isn't only for painting your room! You can also use it to paint a fun, mod pillow. Yay for masking tape!

What Do I Need?

- ¾ yard of patterned fabric, at least 54˝ wide (I like gingham for this project.)

- Removable-ink pen

- Ruler

- 1˝-wide masking tape

- Drop cloth or paper to cover surface

- Fabric paint

- Sponge brush for stenciling

- Old towel or pressing cloth

- Iron

SPECIAL SKILLS

- Using an Iron (page 27)

We need to start by cutting our front pillow panel.

1. Cut a 20″ × 20″ square of patterned fabric.

2.

Using the ruler and removable-ink pen, mark 4 columns, each measuring 5″ wide.

3.

Do the same thing but across the fabric in 4 rows, 5″ wide. Let's call each of these sections blocks.

4.

Using the block corners as your guide, apply the center of the masking tape to the center of the lower right corner, and run it to the top center of the first block.

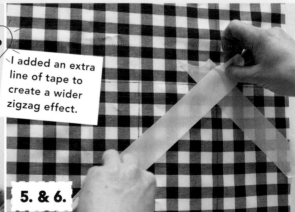

TIP
I added an extra line of tape to create a wider zigzag effect.

5. & 6.

Do the opposite with the next piece of tape to create a zigzag effect.

Continue until you have made 4 lines of taped zigzags across the fabric square.

7.

Iron the panel to remove any ink.

8.

Trim off any overhanging masking tape to make sharp lines.

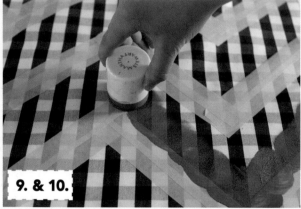

9. & 10.

Lay the pillow front on a flat surface on top of a drop cloth or paper.

Using the sponge stenciling brush, apply the paint, making sure to use a tapping up-and-down motion around the masking tape area.

11.

Leave the pillow front to dry for about an hour before removing the tape.

12.

Wait another hour; then cover the painted area with an old towel or pressing cloth, and iron the design.

This will heat set the paint, and you're ready to finish the pillow.

Time to Make the Pillows!

Now that you have created the pillow fronts, it's time to make the pillows!

What Do I Need?

- The remaining piece of fabric
- Pinking shears
- 20˝ pillow form, 1 for each pillow
- Basic Supplies (page 14)

Prepare the Pieces

You have already cut your front pillow panel. Now cut 2 pieces of fabric 15˝ × 20˝ for the pillow back.

SPECIAL SKILLS

- Sewing Terms (page 30)

Let's Make It!

1.

2.

On a pillow back piece, fold over the edge of a long side about ½″. Iron along this fold.

Fold it over again, iron the fold, and pin it in place.

Repeat this with the second back piece.

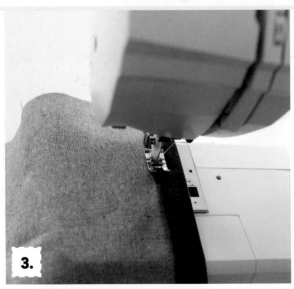

3.

4. Lay the pillow front faceup, and lay a back piece facedown on top of the front piece. Be sure to line up the raw edges along the top, bottom, and one side.

Sew down the fold on both pieces. Try to sew close to the edge of the first fold.

5.

6.

Now lay the second back piece facedown on the stack. This time, make sure that the piece is lined up with the other side of the pillow front. The 2 back pieces will overlap with the hemmed edges toward the center.

Pin everything in place.

7.

8.

Sew around all 4 sides, with the edge of the presser foot on the edge of the fabric.

Trim the corners and trim around the edges with pinking shears to prevent fraying. Turn the pillow right side out.

9. Iron the pillow cover.

10. Insert the pillow form.

Voila! How easy was that? Time to make a whole stack of pillows for your space!

Cross-Stitch Heart Art

What Do I Need?

- Gingham or another check fabric
- Embroidery hoop (I used a 14″ hoop.)
- Removable-ink pen
- Embroidery floss or yarn
- Embroidery needle
- Ribbon
- Scissors
- Patience!

SPECIAL SKILLS
- Hand Sewing (page 28)
- Sewing Terms (page 30)

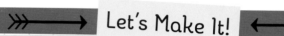

Let's Make It!

1. Cut a piece of gingham fabric a few inches larger than the size of the embroidery hoop. I am using a 14″ hoop, so I am cutting a square of gingham measuring 20″ × 20″.

TIP Keep in mind that the size of your heart will depend on the size of the squares on the gingham. The squares in my fabric are ¼″ × ¼″.

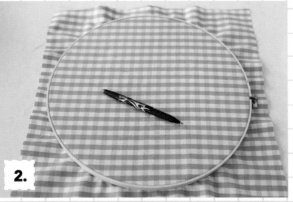

2. Hoop your gingham fabric. Make sure that both the fabric and the hoop are nice and tight.

Who doesn't love hearts?
I believe there can never be
too much love hanging around.
That's why this cross-stitch piece
is the perfect room accessory to
make you feel the love!

Cross-Stitch Heart Art

3.

Look at the cross-stitch pattern (below), and transfer it to the gingham fabric by marking the crosses with your removable-ink pen. I used 4 small squares as a check for each cross stitch.

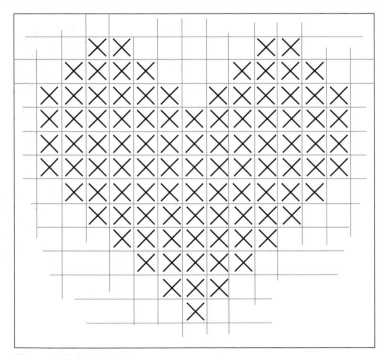

Cross-stitch heart pattern

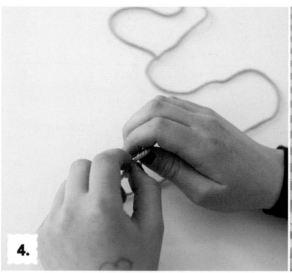

4. Start out by threading your embroidery needle with an arm's length of floss (or yarn). Tie a knot in the end.

5. You are going to work in rows. The first part of the row will be sewing half stitches.

Bring your needle up from behind the fabric and through the lower left-hand corner of the check. I used 4 small squares as one check.

6. Sew down, pushing your needle through the fabric on the upper right-hand side of the check. Continue doing this until you have completed a full row.

7. The next thing to do is to work backward to complete the cross. This time we are sewing the stitches from the lower right-hand corner of the check to the upper left-hand corner of the check.

TIP

Remember: Make sure that you take a break and check the diagram. It is easy to lose track of the stitches.

8.

When you have completed the row, it is time to start on the next one. Continue doing this until you have completed the heart.

9.

10.

On your final stitch, take the needle through to the back again, and tie a final knot close to the fabric.

When you have finished the heart, trim any loose threads, and trim the excess fabric from the hoop.

tip

If you run out of floss while you are working, just take the thread to the back of the fabric and tie a knot close to the fabric. Thread the needle with a new piece of floss, tie a knot in the end, and keep on going.

11. Hang the hoop from a ribbon and you have an instant love artwork.

It is fun to experiment with different-sized hoops and gingham. Hang them all together for a whole room o' love!

Mod Stamped
STORAGE BASKETS

What Do I Need?

- Canvas fabric measuring 55″ × 25″*

- Fabric square, measuring 15″ × 15″*

- Dishwashing sponge

- Scissors

- Large piece of paper or drop cloth

- Fabric paint

- Old towel

- Milk crate (or two!)

- Basic Supplies (page 14)

Size varies depending on the size crate you use. See Prepare the Pieces (page 89).

SPECIAL SKILLS

- Using an Iron (page 27)
- Sewing Terms (page 30)

Let's Paint It!

1.

Using a sharp pair of scissors, cut the sponge into a fun shape.

2.

Lay the canvas fabric on top of a large piece of paper or a drop cloth.

From milk crate to awesome storage basket, this project will have you stockpiling forgotten milk crates to create a storage system that even the milkman will be jealous of!

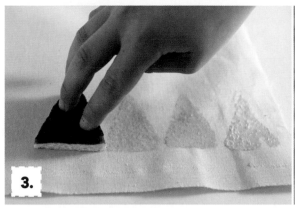

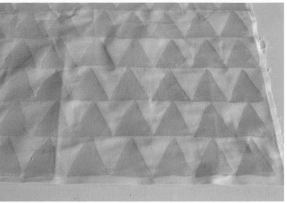

Using the sponge, apply painted shapes all over your piece of canvas.

Wait for the paint to dry for a couple of hours.

4. Lay an old towel over the fabric, and iron the canvas. This will heat set the paint.

Prepare the Pieces

1. Using a measuring tape, measure from the base of the crate all the way over the top and down to the inside base. Mine measures around 21½˝. Add 1˝ to this, for a total height of 22½˝.

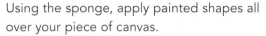 **FYI** Milk crates can come in different sizes. I am working with a milk crate that measures 10½˝ tall and 51˝ all around.

2. Next, take your measuring tape, and measure all the way around the sides. Mine measures 51˝. Add 1½˝ to this, and you'll have a final measurement of 52½˝.

3. Now take a measurement of the inside dimensions of the bottom of the crate. Mine measures 11¾˝ × 11¾˝. Add 1˝ to each measurement and you'll have the final inside measurement; mine is 12¾˝ × 12¾˝.

1. Cut the painted canvas to measure the height and width you calculated. (My measurements are 52½˝ wide × 22½˝ tall.)

2. Cut a square of fabric to measure the inside dimensions you calculated. (My measurements are 12¾˝ × 12¾˝.)

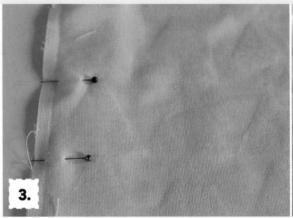

3.

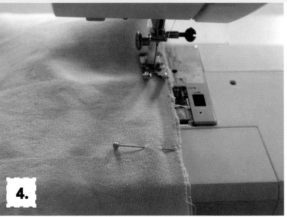

4.

Fold the painted canvas piece in half, and pin the short ends together. Make sure the fabric is folded with right sides together.

Sew with the edge of the fabric along the edge of the presser foot.

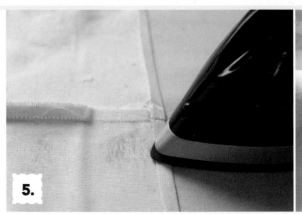

5.

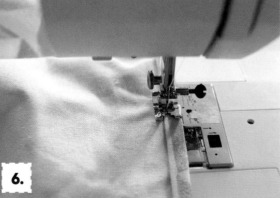

6.

On the bottom of the canvas piece, fold up the edge ¼˝ to the wrong side, and iron. Fold it up another ¼˝, iron again, and pin in place.

Sew nice and close to the folded edge.

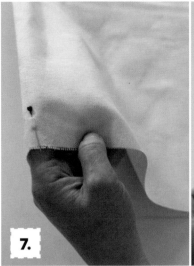

7.

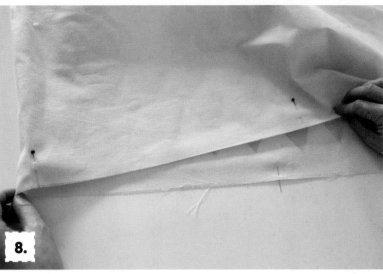

8.

Mark the 4 quarter points of the fabric tube. To do this, first fold the tube in half with the seam on one side of the half. Mark the folded edge with a pin. The pin is the halfway point.

Now fold the tube in half the other way, matching the seam and pin marks in the center. Mark the folded sides with pins. These are your quarter points.

9.

10.

With the right side of the fabric tube and right side of the square together, pin the square corners to the pinned quarter points on the tube.

Pin around all the other sides of the square, attaching it to the bottom of the tube.

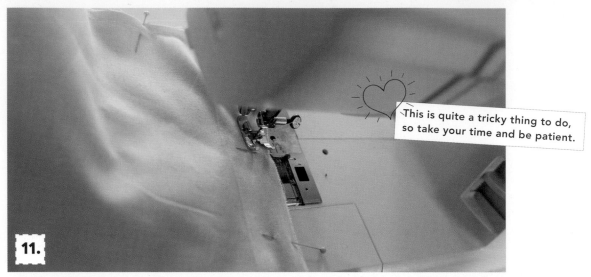

This is quite a tricky thing to do, so take your time and be patient.

11.

Sew carefully around each edge, remembering to move the fabric out of the way when you need to pivot around the corner.

12. Turn the tube right side out, and slide the square bottom into the crate. It is going to seem too high for the crate!

13.

Now all you need to do is fold the upper part of the tube over the front of the crate.

All done. Great job!

A Little Bit Boho

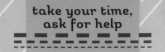

HIPPY DIPPY
Bed Canopy

What Do I Need?

- 5½ yards of a thin 60″-wide cotton fabric
- Wood embroidery hoop measuring 23″ across
- Pencil
- Sashing cord or clothesline
- Basic Supplies (page 14)

SPECIAL SKILLS

- Using an Iron (page 27)
- Sewing Terms (page 30)

Prepare the Pieces

1. Cut 2 fabric panels, each measuring 55″ × 84″.

2. Cut 10 fabric strips measuring 4½″ × 27″.

→→→ **Let's Make It!** ←←←

1.

For each of the fabric panels, fold in a long edge of the fabric 1″ to the wrong side, and iron. Fold in another 1″, and iron again.

2. & 3.

Pin in place.

Do the same with the other long side.

Turn your bedroom into a dreamy hideaway with this easy-peasy bed canopy. I feel relaxed just thinking about it!

Hippy Dippy Bed Canopy

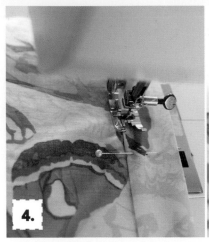

4.

Sew nice and close to the first folded edge down each long side of the panels.

5.

Fold in the top and bottom edges of the fabric 1″ to the wrong side, and iron. Fold in another 1″, iron again, and pin in place.

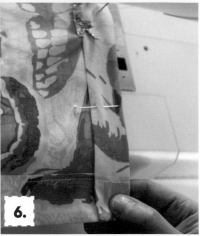

6.

Once again, you will be sewing nice and close to the first folded edge down each top and bottom edge of the panels.

Your panels should measure approximately 51″ × 80″.

Now for the Ties

1.

Take one of the strips, and fold it in half lengthwise, wrong sides together. Iron it nice and flat.

2. & 3.

Open the strip, fold each of the short ends in about ¼″ to the wrong side, and iron.

Fold each of the long ends in about ¼″ to the wrong side, and iron.

4. Refold the entire strip in half again, and iron.

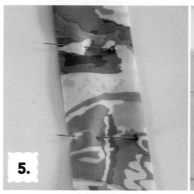

5.

You may want to pin down the open edges, especially if you are using a thin fabric.

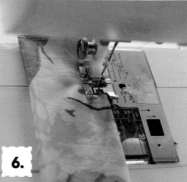

6.

Sew nice and close to the folded edge down both the short ends and the long side.

7. Repeat Steps 1–6 to make 10 ties.

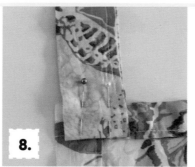

8.

Fold a tie in half, and pin the folded end onto one top corner of a panel. Repeat to pin a folded tie to the other top corner of the panel.

9. Now measure with your ruler to find the halfway point of the top of the panel, and pin another tie.

10. Next, find the halfway point between the end and middle ties, and pin your fourth tie.

Do the same on the other side with the final tie.

11. Sew along the folded edge of each tie. Make sure to backstitch at the beginning and end.

12. Repeat Steps 8–11 with the other panel.

tip

Backstitching is crucial to keep your stitching nice and tight!

1. Mark the quarter points of the hoop with a pencil. This is where we will be tying the cord to hang the canopy. The cord needs to be perfectly positioned so the canopy does not tilt unevenly.

2.

Tie a long length of sashing cord or clothesline with a triple knot at each of the pencil points.

3. Hold the canopy up from the cord, and adjust the cord lengths until the hoop is hanging perfectly level.

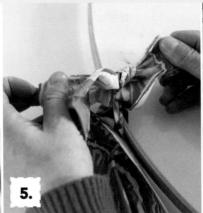

5.

Tie the panels to the embroidery hoop. Make the knots loose enough to be able to slide them on the hoop so you can adjust the panels later.

Ready to hang!

4.

Tie a knot in the top.

tip

The length of the cord will depend on how high your ceiling is. This is a good time to ask for help from an adult.

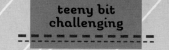

BOHO LOVE
Lampshade

What Do I Need?

- Drum lampshade, any size that will look good with your lamp base

- Large sheet or roll of paper (Kraft paper works well!)

- Pencil

- Fabric scraps

- Hot glue gun

- Trim galore (pompoms, tassels, fringe)

- Basic Supplies (page 14)

SPECIAL SKILLS

- Using a Hot Glue Gun (page 22)
- Using Patterns (page 25)
- Using an Iron (page 27)
- Sewing Terms (page 30)

Let's Make the Pattern!

1. Lay out a large piece of paper. Roll the lampshade on the paper before you start tracing, just to make sure that the paper is big enough for the pattern.

When you have made sure that the paper is big enough, lay the lampshade on its side on the paper, with the seam touching the paper. Make a mark with your pencil; this will be the starting point.

Gently roll the lampshade along the paper, tracing along the bottom edge with your pencil until you get back to the seam.

Imagine how great it will be to have a truly one-of-a-kind lampshade designed by ... that's right ... *you*! This easy and fun project will be sure to shine the light on your super craftiness!

4. Mark the seam on the paper again. This will be the ending point.

5. Go back to the starting point, and lay the lampshade seam in position. Do the same tracing again, only this time, trace along the top edge of the lampshade.

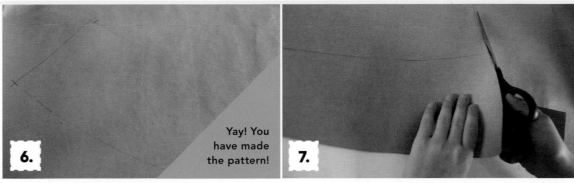

Yay! You have made the pattern!

6. Draw a line on both ends of the pattern, joining the top line to the bottom line.

7. Cut out the pattern.

Let's Make It!

There is no exact design for this lampshade. This is a project for you to get creative and design your own work of art.

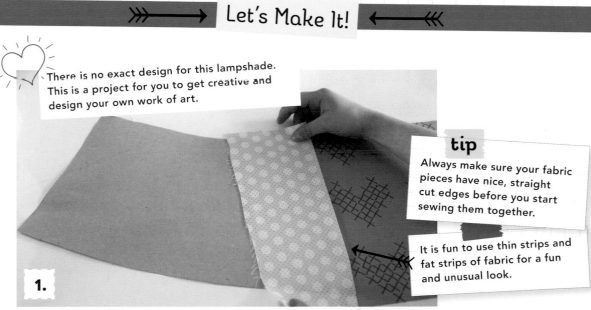

tip
Always make sure your fabric pieces have nice, straight cut edges before you start sewing them together.

It is fun to use thin strips and fat strips of fabric for a fun and unusual look.

1. Choose a few fabric pieces to use to create the design. Lay them out on top of the pattern, and make sure that they are big enough.

Boho Love Lampshade

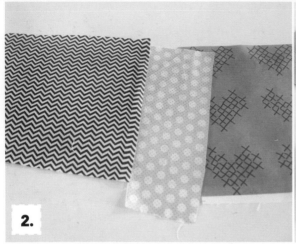

2.

I like to lay out all the pieces side by side before I start sewing them together.

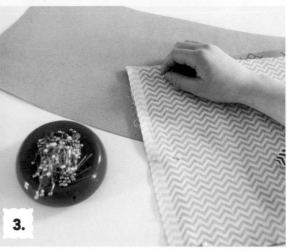

3.

Start by laying your first 2 strips right sides together, and pin down the side.

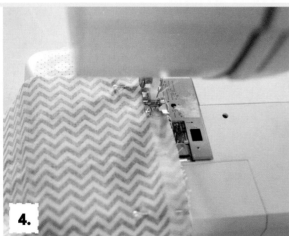

4.

Sew down the side, with the edge of the presser foot on the edge of the fabric.

5.

Iron the strips open.

6. Attach the third piece in the same way.

7. Continue until you have sewn all the pieces together. The piece needs to be bigger than the pattern piece. Add extra strips if you need to.

8. Iron the entire piece.

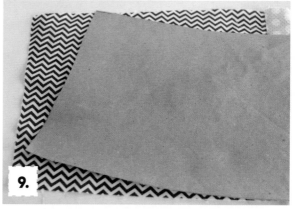

Lay the pattern piece on top of the sewn fabric piece, and pin in place.

Cut out the fabric piece, following the paper pattern and cutting the fabric at least ¼″ longer on one short end.

11. Wrap the fabric piece around the lampshade to check the fit. It's okay if it hangs over the edge a little; we will be able to trim it down later.

Hot glue one end to the seam of the lampshade. You only need a little bit of glue.

Tightly wrap the fabric around the shade until it meets up and slightly overlaps the start.

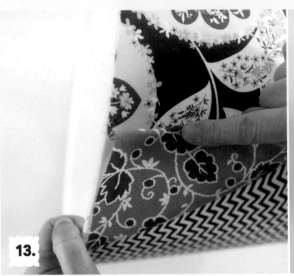

13.

Fold over the raw edge a little, and use a few drops of hot glue to hold it in place.

14.

Carefully trim any overhanging fabric from the edges.

tip

Start adding trim!
Here is where you get to be even more crafty and clever.
You can choose to add trim to the top, the bottom, or both!

15.

Use a little bead of hot glue to attach all the trim. Remember, a little glue goes a long way!

How cool is this lampshade! It will be sure to light up your day (and your room of course!).

GROOVY APPLIQUÉ
Floor Rug

What Do I Need?

- A flat woven floor rug (Mine measures 31″ × 55″.)
- ¼ yard of felt
- ¼ yard of fusible web
- Parchment paper
- Removable-ink pen
- Embroidery floss
- Embroidery needle
- Basic Supplies (page 14)

SPECIAL SKILLS

- Using Fusible Web (page 22)
- Using Patterns (page 25)
- Using an Iron (page 27)
- Hand Sewing (Blanket Stitch, page 29)

Prepare the Pieces

1. Fold a piece of parchment paper in half. Position the heart pattern (page 166) onto the parchment paper along the fold. Trace and cut out the heart.

2. Use the parchment paper pattern to draw hearts on the paper side of the fusible web.

3. Iron the fusible web onto the felt piece.

No more cold toes for you with this very groovy appliqué floor rug. You will be jumping for joy over your new hand-sewing skills!

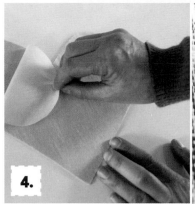

4. Cut out the hearts, and remove the backing paper.

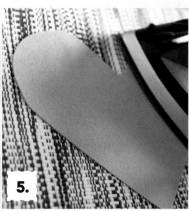

5. Iron in place on the end of the rug.

6. Mark little dots evenly spaced on the edge of the heart with the removable-ink pen. This will help you to keep your stitches all the same size.

Let's Make It!

1. Cut a nice, long piece of embroidery floss. Be sure to tie a knot in the end.

2. Bring the needle up from behind into a marked dot. I find it easiest to start on one side of the bottom point of the heart.

3. Push the needle down into the next dot, and then bring it up again just above the edge of the felt, directly above the dot. As you pull the needle through, you will see a loop.

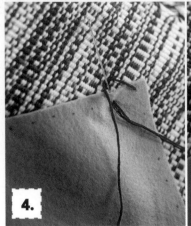

4. Before you pull the floss all the way through, you should put your needle through the loop and pull.

5. Keep doing this all the way around the heart until you are back where you started.

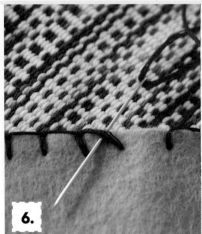

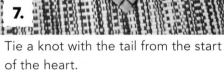

6. When you get back to where you started, thread the needle through the first angled stitch, and bring the needle to the back of the rug.

7. Tie a knot with the tail from the start of the heart.

Now do this again with the other hearts.

How cute is this rug? It will definitely make you go shoeless in your room!

I LOVE YOU
Wall Art

Finished size: 16″ × 20″

What Do I Need?

- Fun, groovy fabric measuring at least 24″ × 28″
- Felt scraps
- Parchment paper
- Fusible web
- Stretched canvas measuring 16″ × 20″
- Staple gun
- Basic supplies (page 14)

SPECIAL SKILLS

- Using Fusible Web (page 22)
- Using Patterns (page 25)
- Using a Staple Gun (page 26)
- Using an Iron (page 27)

Prepare the Pieces

1. Cut your groovy fabric to 24″ × 28″.

2. Trace the letters and heart (page 174) onto a piece of parchment paper. Cut out the pieces.

3. Trace the heart, and trace the letters backward, onto the paper side of the fusible web.

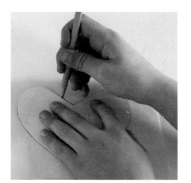

4. Iron the fusible web onto the felt.

5. Cut out the heart and letters.

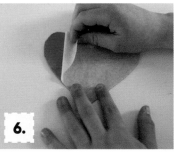

6. Peel away the paper backing, and iron the letters and heart to the center of the fabric piece.

Shout it from the rooftops ... or simply make a sign. This special wall art will teach you some awesome new sewing skills.

1.

Now we are ready to sew around the letters. Sew nice and close to the edge.

2. Once you have finished the design, cut the fabric piece to 20″ × 24″, making sure that the words are perfectly centered on the fabric.

3. Place the fabric facedown on a flat surface.

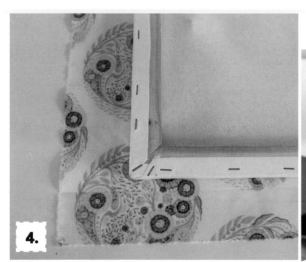

4.

Center the canvas on top, and start folding in each side tightly.

5.

With help from an adult, use the staple gun to put an anchoring staple on the center of each edge of the folded-in fabric.

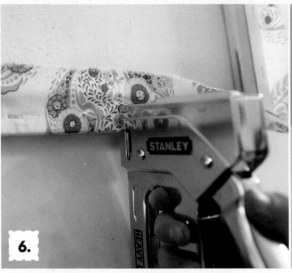

6. Staple on either side of those initial anchoring staples.

Time to tackle the corners.

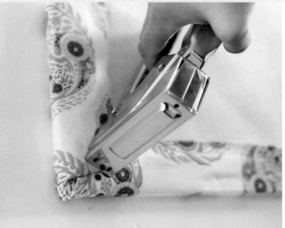

7. First, pull the fabric over the corner.

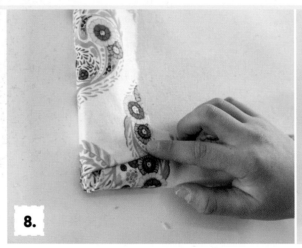

8. Next, gently fold in the fabric on either side of that corner, and staple into place.

9. Continue stapling around the rest of the canvas until everything is nice and secure.

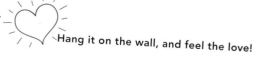

Hang it on the wall, and feel the love!

SEWN FLOWER
Chandelier

Finished size: approximately 14″ tall × 12″ wide

What Do I Need?

- Felt scraps for flowers
- ½ yard green felt for vines
- Parchment paper
- Hot glue gun
- 2 embroidery hoops, 10″ and 12″
- Twine
- Basic Supplies (page 14)

SPECIAL SKILLS

- Using a Hot Glue Gun (page 22)
- Using Patterns (page 25)

Prepare the Pieces

1. Trace the flower patterns (pages 167–169) onto parchment paper.

2. Trace the small and large leafy vine patterns (pages 168 and 169) on parchment paper, joining the pattern pieces as indicated.

3. Cut out the patterns.

4. Cut the flowers out of felt scraps to make a large pile of flowers in different colors and shapes. I used approximately 45 flowers.

5. Cut 3 small leafy vines and 3 large leafy vines, for 6 total.

I love all things whimsical and flowery! This hanging chandelier will make you feel happy and springy!

Sewn Flower Chandelier

The Vine

1.

Hot glue the vine sections to the outsides of the embroidery hoops. (We are using only the inside parts of the embroidery hoops.)

2. Trim off any excess felt vine; you may want to overlap the ends. That would look cute!

tip
Make sure the hanging bits of the vine are on the bottom edge of the hoop.

The Flowers

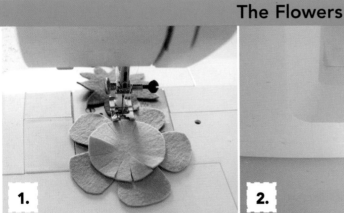

1.

I stacked some of the flowers to add a bit of fun. It is really up to you!

2.

Beginning with a backstitch, feed the flowers through the sewing machine one at a time. Make sure that you are always sewing on a flower; you need to always have felt going through the machine.

3. Once you have sewn halfway through one flower, you should have the next flower ready to go.

4. Continue sewing until all the flowers are in one really, really long strand.

1.

Find the 4 quarter points on the 10″ and 12″ hoops, and mark them with pins.

2.

Measure a 10″ length of flowers, and snip the thread between the flowers. We will want 4 of these 10″ strands.

3.

Hot glue the top flower of each strand at each pinned point on the smaller (top) hoop.

tip

Make sure the hanging bits of the vine are hanging down.

4.

Next, pin the bottom flower of each strand to the pinned points on the larger (bottom) hoop.

5.

Once all the strands are pinned to the larger (bottom) hoop, hold the hoops up to check that they are level.

6.

8.

When it looks good, carefully remove each pin, and put a spot of hot glue exactly where the pin was, gluing the strand in place.

7. Find the halfway points between the flower strands on the bottom hoop, and mark with 4 pins.

Cut 2 flower strands, each measuring around 20˝ long.

9. Pin one strand so that it hangs from one pinned point to the opposite pinned point. Do the same with the other strand. Check that everything is hanging level, and make adjustments, if needed.

10.

11.

Finally, we want to attach 4 pieces of twine at quarter points around the top hoop.

Hot glue the strands at the pin spots.

Cut 4 lengths of twine 16˝, and simply knot them at the quarter points.

12.

Hold up the chandelier by the twine, and make sure it is hanging level. Then join the 4 pieces together, and tie a knot.

Now is the time to add any little sweet butterflies, birds, or pompoms to your gorgeous chandelier.

Don't you just love it?

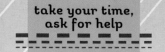
PARTY MOUSE
Doorstop

Finished size: 10″ without the hat

What Do I Need?

- 1/3 yard, or 4 sheets 9″ × 12″, of purple or gray felt for mouse
- Felt scrap for party hat
- Polyfill stuffing
- Rice
- White and black button thread
- Pale pink fabric marker
- Removable-ink pen
- 2 black seed beads
- 1 yard of embroidery floss
- Pompom
- Basic Supplies (page 14)

SPECIAL SKILLS

- Using a Hot Glue Gun (page 22)
- Using Patterns (page 25)
- Using an Iron (page 27)
- Hand Sewing (page 28)
- Sewing Terms (page 30)

Prepare the Pieces

1. Trace the mouse ear, arm, base, and hat patterns (pages 170, 172, and 173) onto parchment paper.

2. Trace the mouse back and front patterns (pages 170–173) onto parchment paper, joining the pattern pieces as indicated.

3. Cut out the patterns.

4. Pin the pattern pieces onto the felt, and cut them out really carefully.

Let's Make It!

The Body

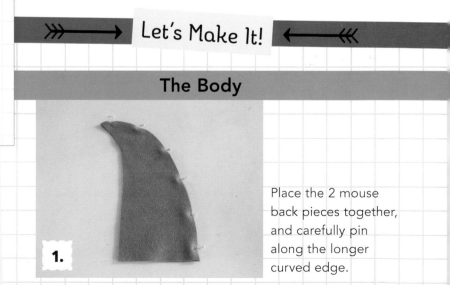

1.

Place the 2 mouse back pieces together, and carefully pin along the longer curved edge.

Say goodbye to that dreary old doorstop and hello to this happy little party mouse! He will work hard to make sure your door is always open! He is a doorstop after all!

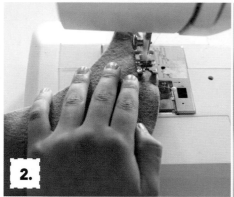

2.

Sew along the curve, with the edge of the foot on the edge of the fabric.

3.

Fold the mouse front piece in half to find the center point of the upper curve. Mark it with a pin.

4. Line up the marked center point of the front piece with the top of the center seam on the back piece, with right sides together.

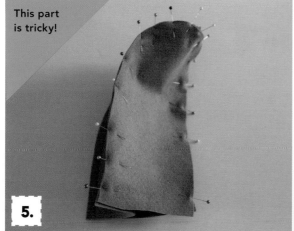

This part is tricky!

5.

Carefully pin the mouse front piece to the mouse back piece. It may look like it is not going to fit; you just have to move it around a little until the edges perfectly match up. Keep pinning until the whole front piece is in place.

6.

Carefully sew all the way around the pinned edges. Be sure to keep the edge of the foot on the edge of the fabric.

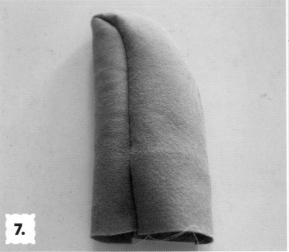

7.

Now turn your mouse right side out, and make sure to push out the top tip for his nose.

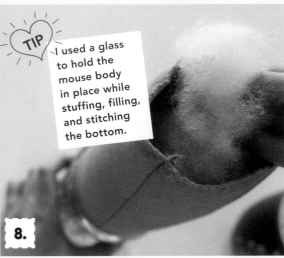

TIP I used a glass to hold the mouse body in place while stuffing, filling, and stitching the bottom.

8.

Stuff your mouse firmly with polyfill stuffing to about halfway up the body.

9.

Fill the rest of the body with rice. Be sure to stop when the rice reaches 2″ from the top.

10. Finish stuffing with polyfill.

11.

Pin the circular felt mouse base in place.

12.

Thread your needle with white button thread. Whipstitch around the circle to attach it to the mouse body. Be sure to start with a knot!

122

1.

Mark the mouse cheeks using the pink fabric marker.

2.

Once the marker has dried, run a hot iron over the cheeks to set the ink.

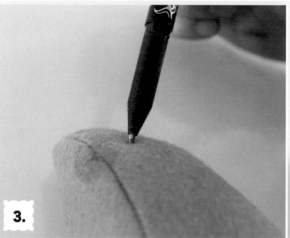

3.

Use the removable-ink pen to mark the eye position. The location is up to you; I like them to be just above the cheeks.

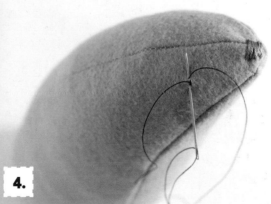

4.

To sew on the eyes I knot a piece of black button thread, and make a small stitch through the mark of the eye.

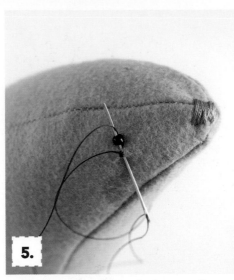

5. Add a bead, and push the needle back to the starting side.

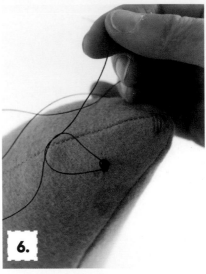

6. Use the starting thread tail to tie a double knot. This will secure the bead in place.

7. Add the second eye in the same way.

8. Draw an upside-down triangle on the nose area.

9. Thread a needle with embroidery floss, and tie a knot in the end.

10. Thread the needle through one side at the top of the triangle and out the other side.

11.

Go back to the starting side, and sew another stitch directly below. Continue doing this until the entire nose is filled. It can be as big or as little as you want it to be. When finished, push the needle all the way through the nose one more time, and trim the floss.

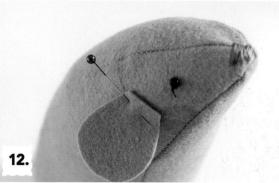

12.

Position the ears in place, and pin.

13.

Whipstitch the ears in place using button thread.

The Rest

1. Position the arms on the body, and pin in place.

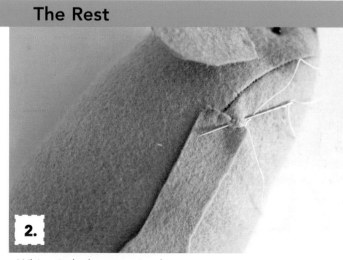

2.

Whipstitch the arms in place.

The Hat

1. Run a bead of hot glue down one edge of the hat triangle.

2. Roll the hat into a cone shape.

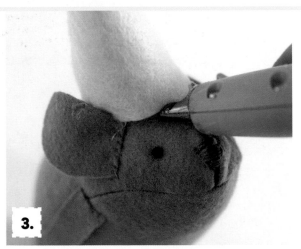

3. Attach to the mouse head with a few drops of glue.

4. Hot glue a pompom on top.

Well done to you!

Remember, there are sure to be many more doors that need a happy mouse doorstop! Reduce the pattern size on the copier to make a whole army of mini mice!

FABRIC TASSEL
Garland

What Do I Need?

- A selection of fat quarters of fabric
- Ruler
- Sharp scissors
- Twine
- Cording

Let's Make It!

They don't all have to be perfect, so don't worry too much!

1.

Using a variety of different fabrics, cut a pile of strips measuring 20″ long and around ¾″–1″ wide. You'll need 90 or more strips.

2. Cut 10 lengths of twine, each 5″.

Every day is a crafty celebration with these fun fabric tassels. Choose some cheery fabric, and start cutting.

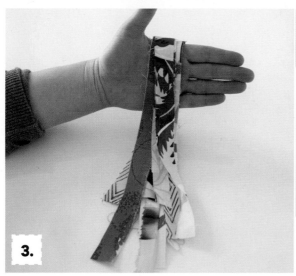

3.

Each tassel will have 9 fabric strips. Start by laying your fabric strips across your hand, adding them one by one with the print facing up.

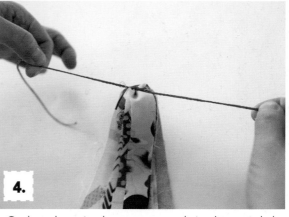

4.

Gather them in the center, and tie them tightly with a piece of twine.

Don't worry if the bottoms look a little uneven; we will give them a haircut at the end.

5.

Repeat this process for all the other strips until you have 10 (or as many as you want) fabric tassels.

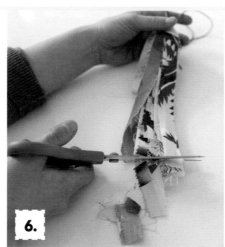

6.

Now give them a little trim so they are all the same length.

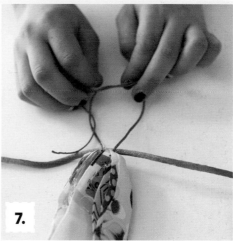

7.

Tie them to a long piece of cording at even intervals. Cut off the excess twine from the tassels.

Hang your awesome garland somewhere fabulous!

No-Sew Ottoman

What Do I Need?

- Small galvanized trash can with lid*

- ½ yard of fabric** (Thicker, decorator-weight fabric works best.)

- Removable-ink pen

- Ruler

- Piece of 1"-thick foam, at least as big as your trash can lid

- High-loft (super fat) batting, at least as big as your trash can lid

- Hot glue gun

- Sharp scissors

I found mine at Home Depot and IKEA.

**You need enough fabric to be as wide as your trash can lid, plus 6".*

SPECIAL SKILLS

- Using a Hot Glue Gun (page 22)

 Let's Make It!

1. Ask for help from an adult to remove the lid handle.

tip

If your trash can does not have a removable handle, ask an adult to flatten the handle with a hammer or mallet. This is definitely grown-up work, so don't be afraid to ask for help!

2. Using the removable-ink pen, trace the trash can lid on the wrong side of your fabric.

Put your feet up on it, sit on it, or just use it as a bedside table. The uses are endless for this ottoman made from a simple trash can. Trash can, you say? Yep, and this one sure is cute!

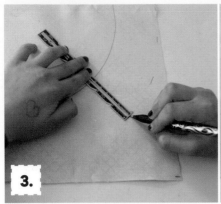

3.

4.

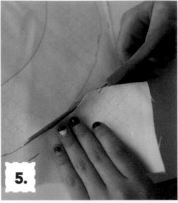

5.

Use a ruler to measure out another 3″ from the drawn circle, and mark all the way around.

Join those marks so that you have another larger circle.

Cut the bigger circle out of the fabric.

6.

7.

Trace the trash can lid on the foam and also on the batting.

Cut out the foam and batting circles.

8. Check that the foam and batting are both the same size and the same size as the lid. Trim where necessary.

9. Lay the fabric circle facedown on a flat surface.

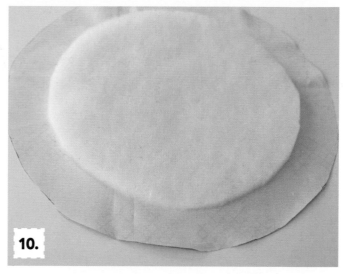

10.

Lay the batting circle centered on the fabric.

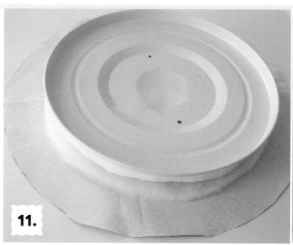

11.

Lay the foam and then the trash can lid facedown on the stack.

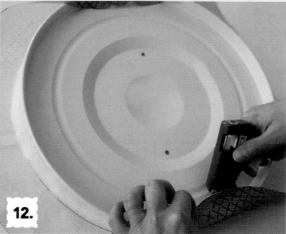

12.

Start by wrapping 2 opposite sides of fabric around the lid, and secure with hot glue.

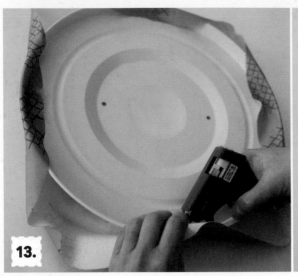

13.

Next, wrap the other 2 sides, securing them with glue. Don't pull too hard, or you will end up with a lumpy, bumpy ottoman top!

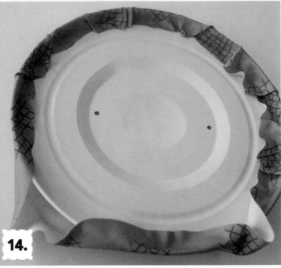

14.

Carefully fold in the fabric between the glued areas, and slowly and carefully glue the rest of the fabric onto the lid.

15.

Cut a fabric circle about the same size as the inside of the lid, and hot glue it onto the inside of the lid. It will cover up all those messy edges.

tip

Use the rim of the trash can to trace the fabric circle for the inside of the lid.

TIP

Use the same fabric or a different fabric for the inside of the lid.

Put the lid back on the can, and put your feet up … you deserve it!

SUPER QUICK
Bunting

What Do I Need?

- A few fat quarters of fabric (You can cut 2 bunting flags from 1 fat quarter!)
- Removable-ink pen
- Ruler
- Twine or cording
- Safety pin
- Basic Supplies (page 14)

SPECIAL SKILLS
- Using an Iron (page 27)
- Sewing Terms (page 30)

Prepare the Pieces

1. Cut a little pile of flag pieces, each measuring 8½″ × 12″.

You can make as many as you like. It all depends on how long you want the bunting to be.

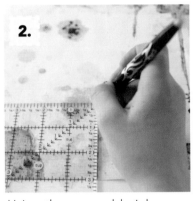

Using the removable-ink pen, mark a 3″-long vertical line centered along the bottom short edge of the flag.

Draw a line from the top of the center line to the lower left-hand corner of the flag.

4. Do the same with the lower right-hand corner.

Remove the drawn triangle shape by cutting along the diagonal lines.

This super quick fabric bunting is so fun to make, you will be stringing it all over the place.

1. Fold the top edge of the flag over ½″ to the wrong side, and iron.

2. Fold over ½″ again, and iron.

3. Pin down the fold.

4. Sew nice and close to the first folded edge.

Do this for all your flags.

Finish Up

1. Lay all the flags out in a line, and arrange the fabrics in a way that you like.

3. Attach a safety pin to the end of the twine or cording, and thread through all the flags.

2. Cut a piece of twine or cording at least 20″ longer than total width of all the flags.

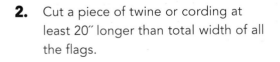

String it up inside or outside for an instant party!

SIMPLE
Binder Cover

What Do I Need?

- ½ yard of laminated cotton fabric
- ½ yard cotton fabric
- Ruler
- Removable-ink pen
- Basic Supplies (page 14)

SPECIAL SKILLS

- Using an Iron (page 27)
- Sewing Terms (page 30)

Prepare the Pieces

1. Using a measuring tape, measure the length of the binder by laying it out flat and measuring from one edge to the other.

2. Add 10″ to the measurement. (My binder is 25″ + 10″ = 35″ length.)

3. Now measure the height of the binder.

Add 1½″ to the measurement. (My binder is 11½″ tall + 1½″ = 13″.)

4. Cut a piece of laminated fabric to measure the height and width you calculated. (My measurements are 35″ × 13″.)

5. Cut a piece of cotton quilting fabric the same size as the laminated fabric.

Sick of looking at your boring, old binder? This project will teach you how to make a statement with your stationery. Yay!

1. Lay the fabric and laminated fabric pieces right sides together.

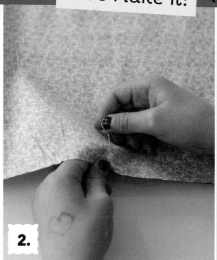

2.

Pin all the way around.

3.

Mark a 4″ line on a short end of the fabric with the removable-ink marker. This is the no-sew zone.

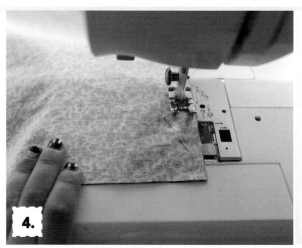

4.

Sew all the way around the 4 sides, with the edge of the presser foot on the edge of the fabric. Remember not to sew in the no-sew zone!

6.

Turn the fabric pieces right side out, and push out the corners.

5. Trim the corners at an angle. Be careful not to cut your stitches.

7. Iron the piece really well on the fabric side; you don't want the laminated side to melt.

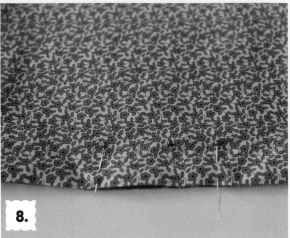

8. Pin the opening closed.

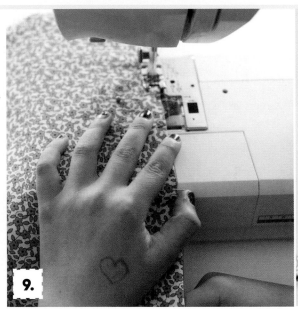

9. Sew the opening closed, sewing nice and close to the edge.

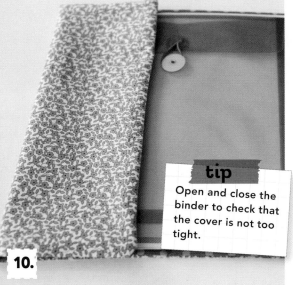

tip
Open and close the binder to check that the cover is not too tight.

10. Lay the binder on the laminated fabric side and fold in the flaps. Make sure the flaps are both the same width and even along the top and bottom edges.

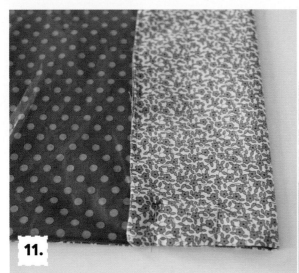

11. Take the binder out, and pin the flaps in place.

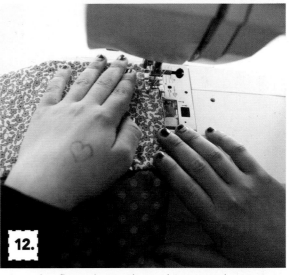

12. Sew the flaps down along the pinned area, sewing close to the edge of the fabric.

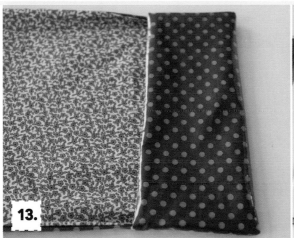

13. Turn the flaps right side out.

14. Slide the binder in.

 You may have the coolest binder cover in school! Now, time to cover all your binders!

Fabric Washi Tape

What Do I Need?

- Scraps of fabric measuring about 20˝ long
- Iron
- Double-sided scrapbooking tape
- Sharp scissors
- Paper clips

SPECIAL SKILLS

- Using an Iron (page 27)

Let's Make It!

1. Start by ironing the fabric pieces super flat; we don't want wrinkly tape!

2. Lay the fabric piece facedown on a flat surface.

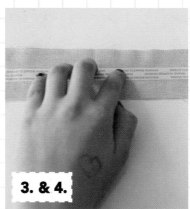

Without touching the sticky side of the tape, lay a precut piece of tape carefully on the wrong side of the fabric, making sure the fabric doesn't get bunched up underneath.

Carefully use your fingers to smooth down the tape so that there are no air bubbles.

3. & 4.

5.

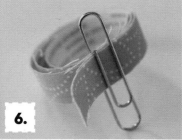

6.

Take a sharp pair of scissors, and carefully cut the fabric, staying right on the tape edge.

When you have cut the length of tape, roll it up, and secure it with a paper clip.

I am a little bit addicted to Washi tape. It's just so cute but kinda hard to find. My solution: make my own! Now you can too! Washi tape looks adorable taped on letters and envelopes for that super personal touch!

Fabric Washi Tape

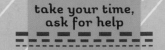

Jewelry Organizer

Finished size: 14¼″ × 27¾″

What Do I Need?

- ½ yard decorator-weight main fabric
- ½ yard decorator-weight backing fabric
- 2 sheets of felt, 9″ × 12″
- Fun-colored thread
- Removable-ink pen
- Packet of snaps
- 18″-long dowel
- Piece of ribbon or twine
- Basic Supplies (page 14)

SPECIAL SKILLS

- Using an Iron (page 27)
- Sewing Terms (page 30)

Prepare the Pieces

1. Cut 1 piece of main fabric measuring 15″ × 30″.

2. Cut 1 piece of backing fabric measuring 15″ × 30″.

3. Cut 4 pockets from felt, each measuring 4½″ × 4½″.

4. Cut 1 pocket from felt measuring 4½″ × 11″.

5. Cut 1 strip of felt measuring 1½″ × 11″.

TIP If you buy 1 yard of decorator fabric, you can use the same fabric on the front and back.

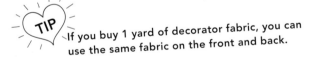

Let's Make It!

1.

Thread the machine with a fun-colored thread, and top-stitch along the top of all your pocket pieces, with the edge of the presser foot on the edge of the fabric.

Jewelry Organizer

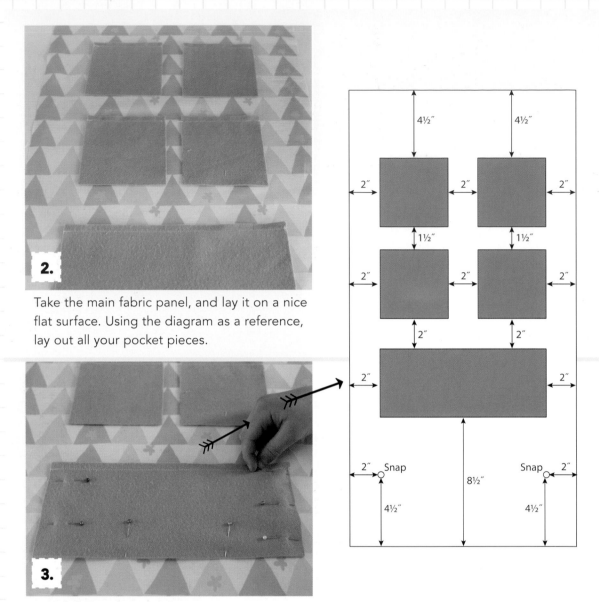

2.

Take the main fabric panel, and lay it on a nice flat surface. Using the diagram as a reference, lay out all your pocket pieces.

3.

Pin all the pockets in place.

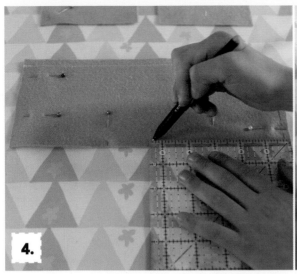

4.

I use my removable-ink pen to draw a line to follow for a ¼″ seam allowance on the pockets. We want this top stitch to be neat, so drawing it on can sometimes make it a little easier.

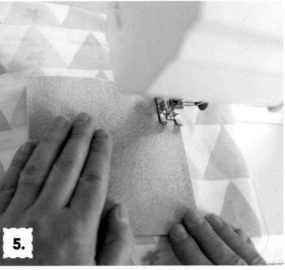

5.

Sew around the pockets, following the drawn line and leaving the tops open.

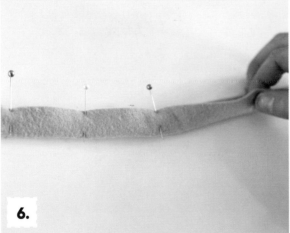

6.

Fold the 1½″-wide strip in half lengthwise, and pin it in place.

7.

Sew down the long edge, with the edge of the presser foot on the edge of the fabric.

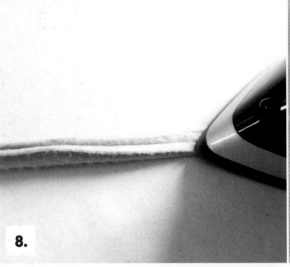

8.

Iron the strip so that the seam is open on the underside.

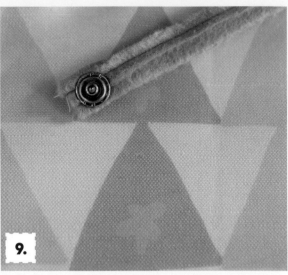

9.

Following the instructions on the snap pack, attach a snap to each end of the ring strip.

10.

To determine the location of the other snap halves, lay the ring strip down on the panel, and make little marks on the panel. Check the measurements from the diagram (page 148) as a reference.

11.

Attach the other half of the snaps to the panel piece.

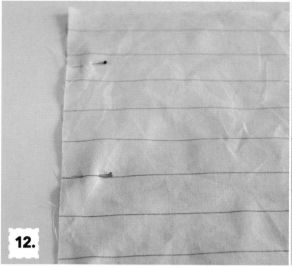

12. Take the front and back panels, and pin them right sides together.

13. Use your removable-ink pen to mark a 4″ line across the top edge to use as the no-sew zone.

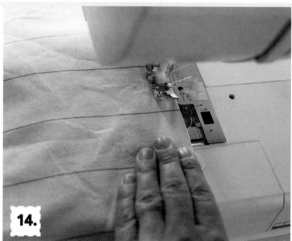

14. Sew all 4 sides, with the edge of the presser foot on the edge of the fabric. Don't forget to leave the no-sew zone open!

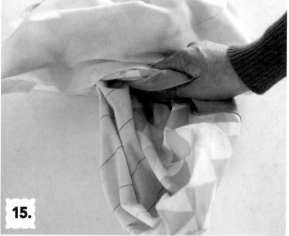

15. Pull the panel right sides out through the opening, and be sure to push out the corners so they look nice and pointy. Give your panel a really good iron.

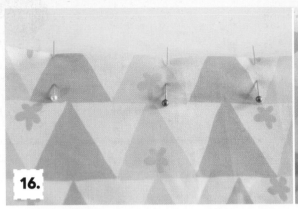

16.

Pin the opening closed.

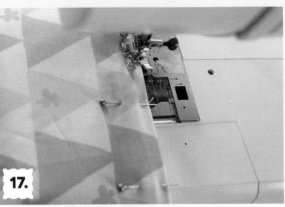

17.

Sew nice and close to the edge along the opening.

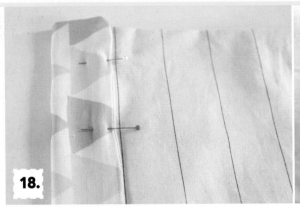

18.

Fold over 1½˝ at the top edge of the fabric panel, and pin in place.

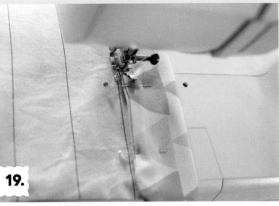

19.

Sew the fold down nice and close to the edge. Remember to backstitch at the beginning and at the end. This creates a casing for your dowel.

20.

Insert the wood dowel into the casing. A little bit should hang out each end. Ask for help to cut it shorter if you need to.

21.

Tie a ribbon or piece of twine to each end of the dowel for hanging, and you are ready to store all your favorite jewelry pieces!

Flashy Trash Can

What Do I Need?

- Hot glue gun
- Variety of yarn
- Small trash can
  (Mine is 9½″ tall.)

SPECIAL SKILLS

- Using a Hot Glue Gun (page 22)

Let's Make It!

1. Starting from the bottom of the trash can, apply a line of hot glue all the way around, and wrap your first row of yarn.

2. Start wrapping tightly around the can. Make sure that the yarn is wrapped really close beside itself rather than on top of itself.

Trash cans should be flashy instead of trashy! Raid your knitting basket for fun yarn to create these one-of-a-kind trash can beauties!

3. Add a few drops of hot glue here and there just to keep things nice and secure.

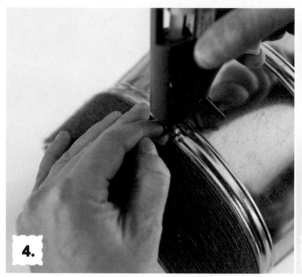

4.

Work in sections. When you have finished one color, carefully glue the end down before you cut it.

5.

Add the next length of yarn, starting in the same spot where you ended the last yarn, and continue wrapping.

6.

When you reach the end, run the hot glue gun all the way around the top of the can to secure your final row.

Isn't your trash can gorgeous?

Try different weights and textures of yarns for a really awesome look!

IN OR OUT
Door Sign

Finished size: 13″ × 9½″

What Do I Need?

- 2 pieces of decorator-weight fabric measuring at least 13″ × 9½″
- Fabric bonding sheet, measuring at least 13″ × 9½″ (I used Phoomph.)
- Parchment paper
- Fusible web
- Felt scraps
- Pinking shears
- Grommet kit
- Twine
- Basic Supplies (page 14)

SPECIAL SKILLS

- Using Fusible Web (page 22)
- Using an Iron (page 27)
- Using a Grommet Kit (follow package instructions)
- Sewing Terms (page 30)

Prepare the Pieces

1. Cut 2 pieces of decorator-weight fabric 13″ × 9½″.

2. Cut 1 piece of the fabric bonding sheet measuring 13″ × 9½″.

3. Using parchment paper, trace the in/out letters (page 175).

4. Cut out the letters.

5. Trace letters backward on the paper side of the fusible web.

6. Iron the fusible web to the felt.

Are you in, or are you out? Let your pesky brother or sister know when your room is open for visitors!

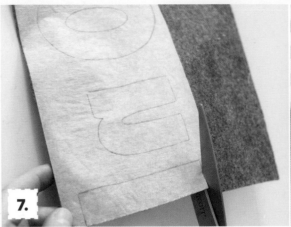

7.

Cut out the letters.

8.

Peel off the backing paper, and iron the letters to the center of each piece of fabric.

tip
Use a fun-colored thread for this. It will look so cute!

1.

Sew nice and close to the edge around each of the letters.

3.

Peel one side of the paper off the fabric bonding sheet.

2. Make a sandwich of layers by laying one piece of fabric facedown on a flat surface.

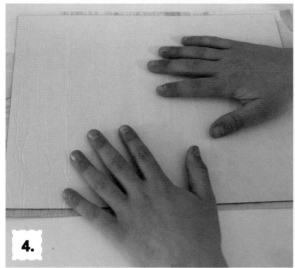

4.

Lay the sticky side down, centered on the fabric.

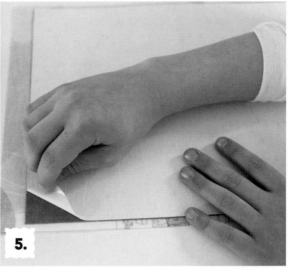

5.

Peel off the other piece of paper from the fabric bonding sheet.

6.

Place the other piece of fabric on top of the stack faceup.

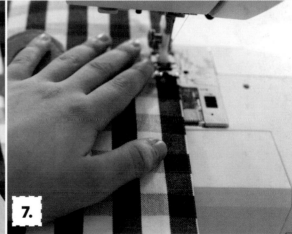

7.

Sew all the way around the sign, with the edge of the presser foot on the edge of the fabric.

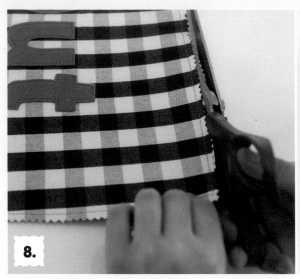

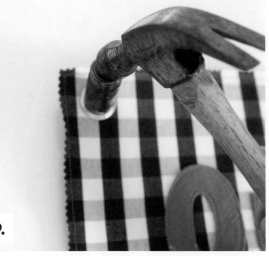

8.

Using pinking shears, cut a cute edge around the sign.

9.

Follow the instructions on the grommet pack, and ask for help to attach a grommet in both upper corners of the sign.

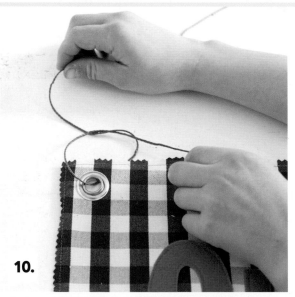

10.

String the sign with twine, hang it on your door, and enjoy your newly found privacy!

Bed Book Storage

What Do I Need?

- ½ yard of upholstery-weight fabric, at least 54″ wide
- 1 fat quarter of fun coordinating fabric
- Removable-ink pen
- Basic Supplies (page 14)

SPECIAL SKILLS

- Using an Iron (page 27)
- Sewing Terms (page 30)

Prepare the Pieces

1. Cut 2 pieces of upholstery-weight fabric 24″ × 16″ for the main part of the bed organizer.

2. Cut 2 pieces of fun coordinating fabric 8½″ × 12″ for the pocket.

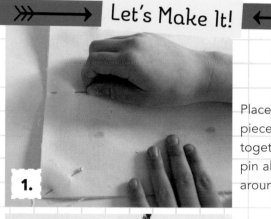

Let's Make It!

1. Place 2 pocket pieces right sides together, and pin all the way around.

2. Mark a 4″ no-sew zone with a removable-ink pen along the long edge at the top of the pocket.

Who knew that making a place to stash your books would be so easy? This fun project will have you channeling your inner bookworm in no time!

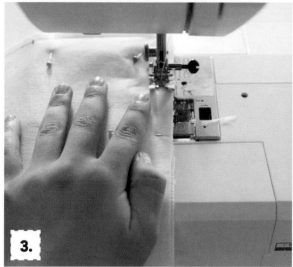

3.

Sew around all 4 sides, with the edge of the foot on the edge of the fabric, but don't forget the no-sew zone!

4.

Pull the pocket right side out through the opening, and iron it nice and flat.

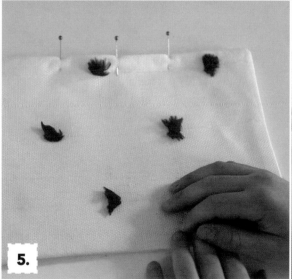

5.

Pin the opening closed.

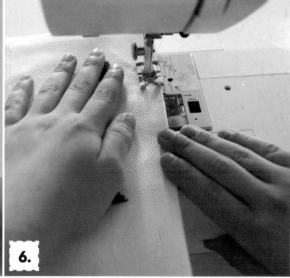

6.

Sew the opening closed by sewing nice and close to the edge along the entire length of the long top edge.

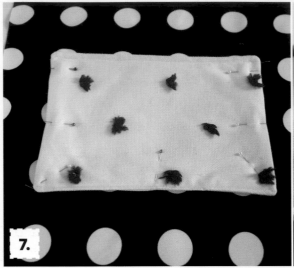

7.

Position the pocket on one of the main fabric panels. Center it 3″ from the short bottom end of the panel, and pin in place. The top of the pocket, with the stitched edge, needs to be facing toward the longer end of the main fabric.

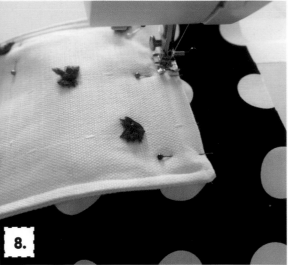

8.

Sew around 3 sides of the pocket. Sew with the edge of the foot on the edge of the fabric, and leave the top of the pocket open.

9.

Put the 2 main fabric panels right sides together, and pin all the way around.

10.

Using the removable-ink pen, mark a 4″ line on the short side as the no-sew zone.

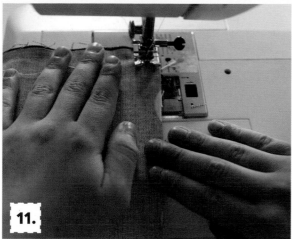

11.

Sew around the 4 sides, making sure not to sew in the no-sew zone.

12.

Turn right sides out, and push out the corners so they look neat and pointy.

Iron the entire piece so it is lovely and flat.

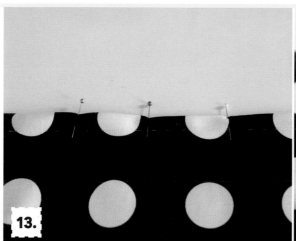

13.

Pin the opening closed.

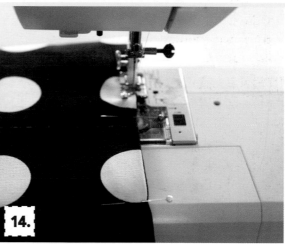

14.

Sew the opening closed by sewing super close to the edge.

15. Tuck the long end of the main fabric between your mattress and box spring or under your chair cushion.

Think of all the books you can read at once with this nifty organizer!

Patterns

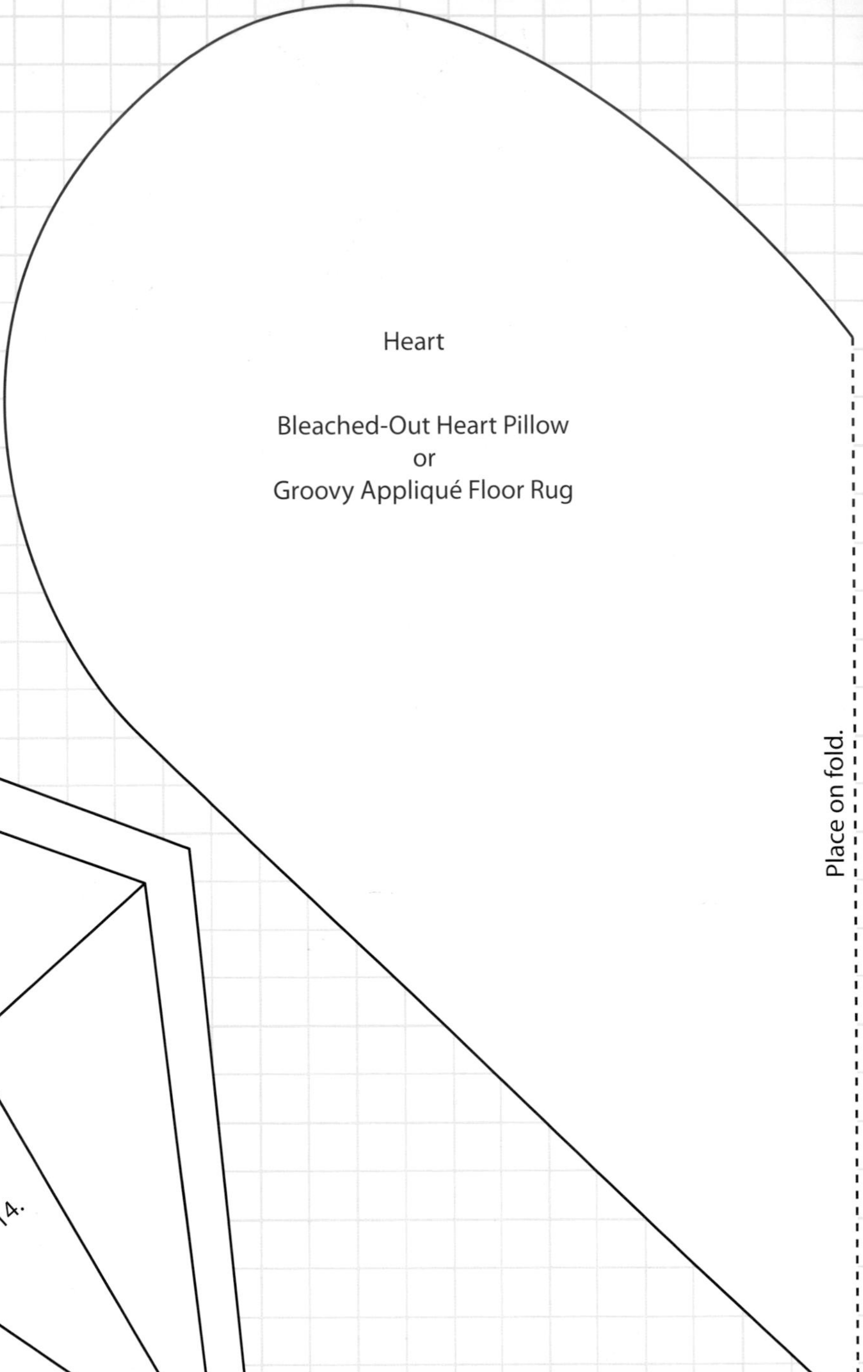

Heart

Bleached-Out Heart Pillow
or
Groovy Appliqué Floor Rug

Place on fold.

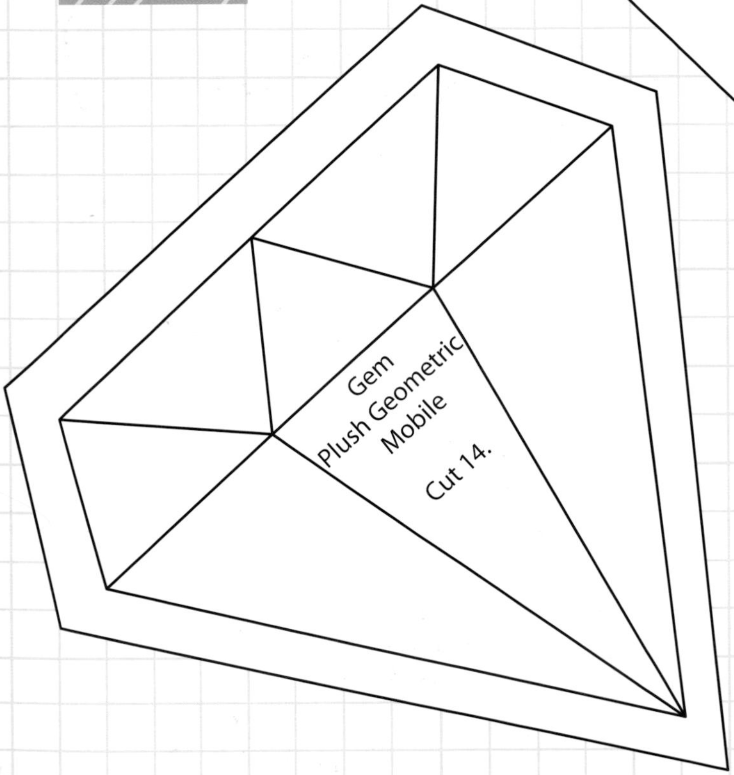

Gem
Plush Geometric
Mobile

Cut 14.

Flower
Sewn Flower
Chandelier

Flower
Sewn Flower
Chandelier

Flower
Sewn Flower
Chandelier

Flower
Sewn Flower Chandelier

Flower
Sewn Flower
Chandelier

Flower
Sewn Flower
Chandelier

Flower
Sewn Flower
Chandelier

Join here.

Small Vine
Sewn Flower Chandelier

Join pattern pieces, and
cut 3 from felt.

Small Vine
Sewn Flower
Chandelier

Join here.

Join pattern pieces, and
cut 3 from felt.

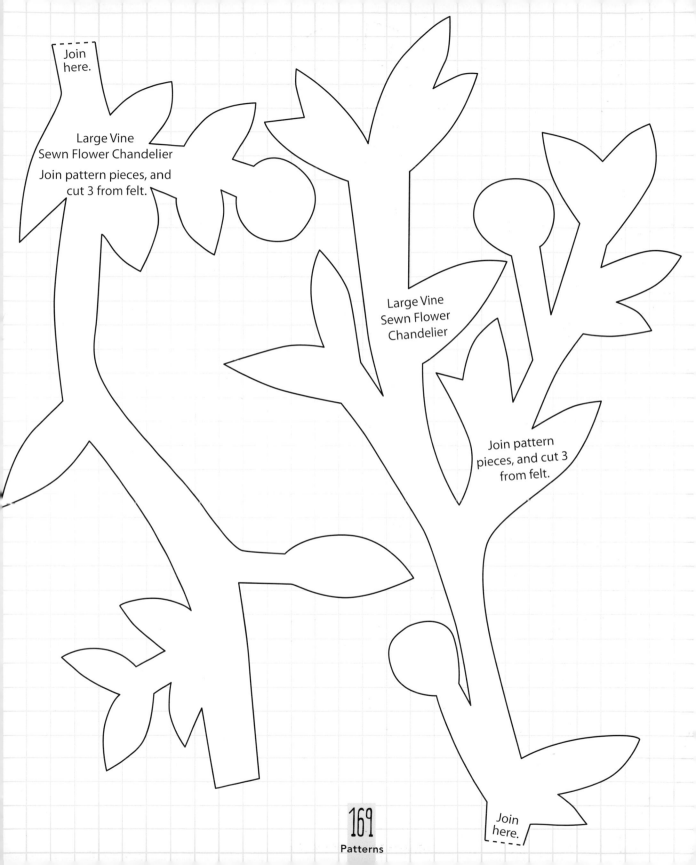

Join here.

Large Vine
Sewn Flower Chandelier

Join pattern pieces, and cut 3 from felt.

Large Vine
Sewn Flower
Chandelier

Join pattern pieces, and cut 3 from felt.

Join here.

Mouse Ear
Party Mouse
Doorstop

Cut 2
from felt.

Mouse Party Hat
Party Mouse Doorstop

Cut 1 from felt.

Mouse Front
Party Mouse Doorstop

Join pattern pieces,
and cut 1 from felt.

Join here.

Join here.

Mouse Front
Party Mouse Doorstop

Join pattern pieces,
and cut 1 from felt.

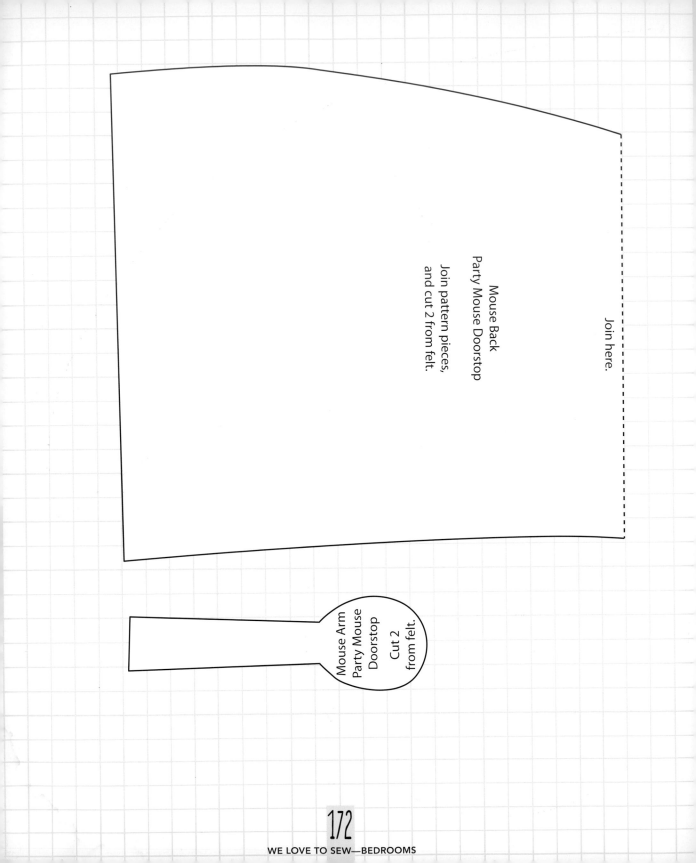

Mouse Back
Party Mouse Doorstop

Join pattern pieces,
and cut 2 from felt.

Join here.

Mouse Arm
Party Mouse
Doorstop

Cut 2
from felt.

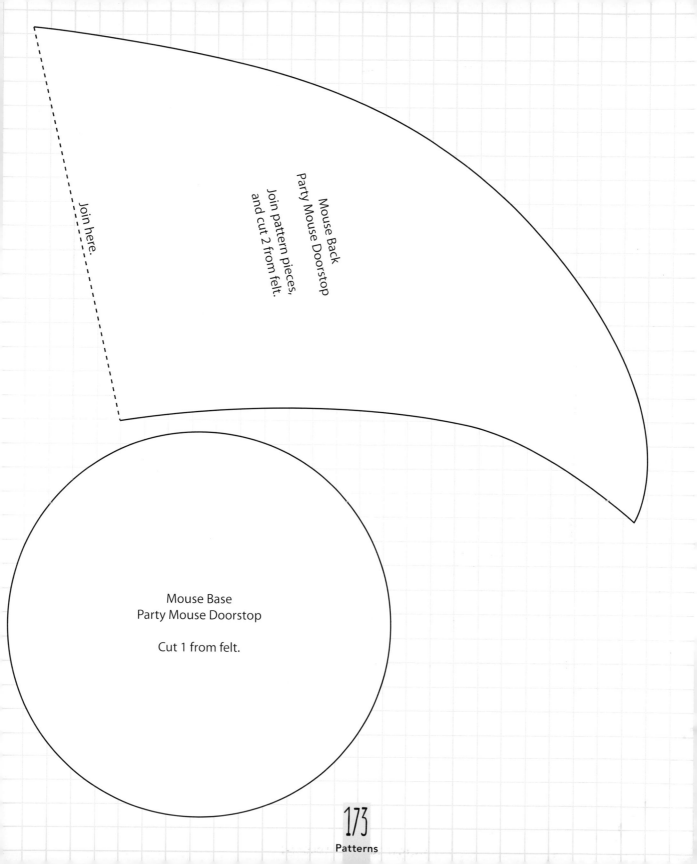

Mouse Back
Party Mouse Doorstop
Join pattern pieces,
and cut 2 from felt.

Join here.

Mouse Base
Party Mouse Doorstop

Cut 1 from felt.

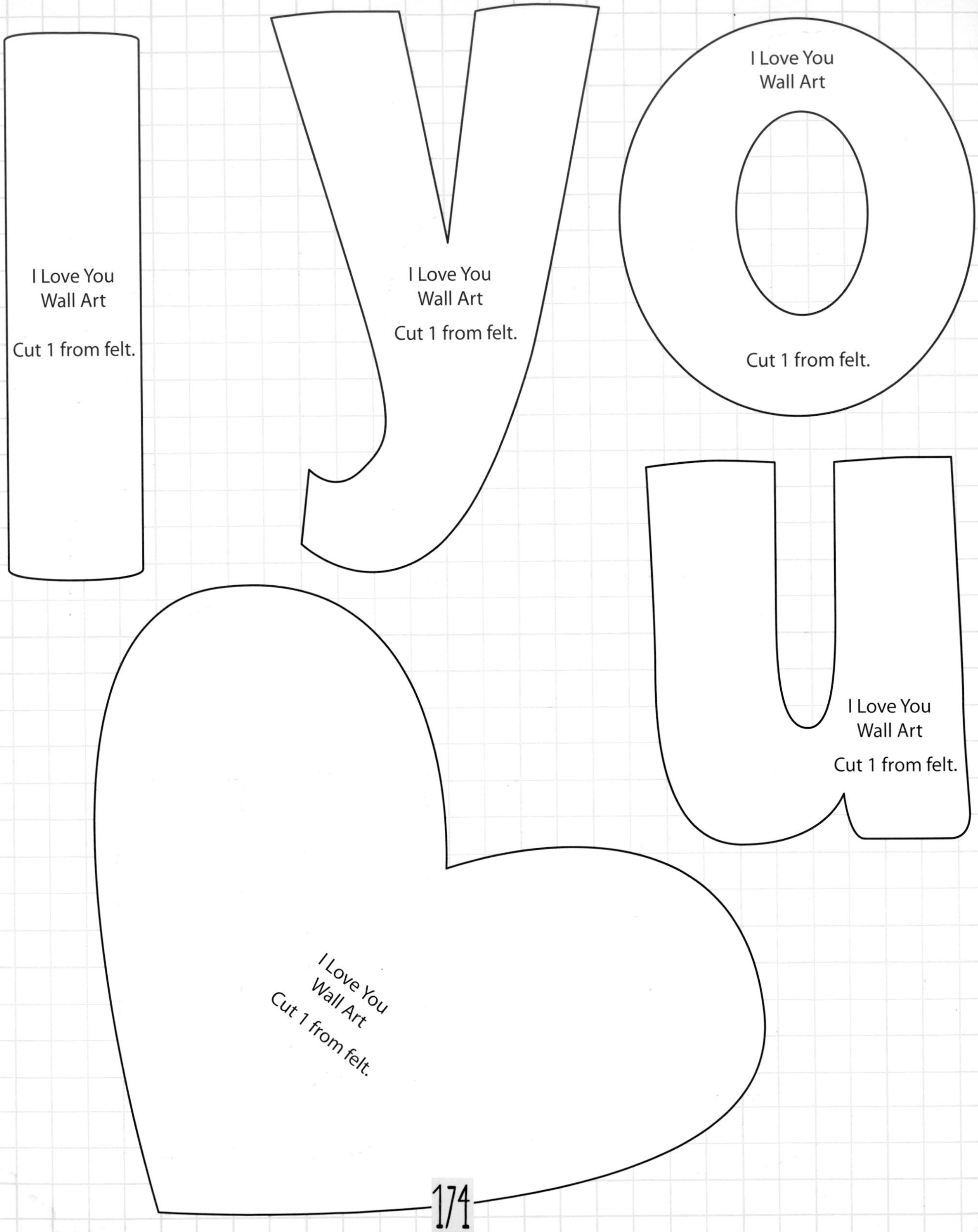

I Love You
Wall Art

Cut 1 from felt.

I Love You
Wall Art

Cut 1 from felt.

I Love You
Wall Art

Cut 1 from felt.

I Love You
Wall Art

Cut 1 from felt.

I Love You
Wall Art
Cut 1 from felt.

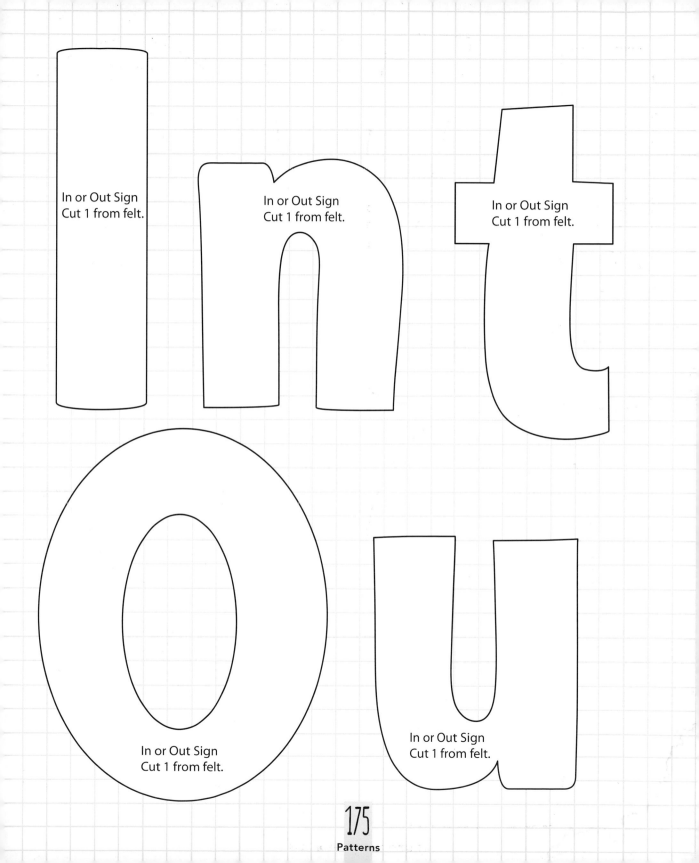

In or Out Sign
Cut 1 from felt.

In or Out Sign
Cut 1 from felt.

In or Out Sign
Cut 1 from felt.

In or Out Sign
Cut 1 from felt.

In or Out Sign
Cut 1 from felt.

Resources

Shops and websites that I love to visit

Coats & Clark   coatsandclark.com

Fabric.com

Hancock Fabrics   hancockfabrics.com

Hawthorne Threads   hawthornethreads.com

Jo-Ann Fabrics   joann.com

Michaels   michaels.com

Purl Soho   purlsoho.com

Super lovely and helpful companies

Denyse Schmidt Quilts   dsquilts.com

Lion Brand Yarns   lionbrand.com

Michael Miller Fabrics   michaelmillerfabrics.com

National Nonwovens   woolfelt.com

Spoonflower   spoonflower.com

Windham Fabrics   windhamfabrics.com

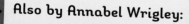

Also by Annabel Wrigley:

About the Author

Annabel is a crafty Aussie mum living in the Virginia countryside. She owns Little Pincushion Studio, where she teaches sewing classes to a creative gang of sweet girls. (And a few clever boys!)

She writes a blog by the same name, where she shares her daily inspirations, class adventures, and thrifty finds.

She lives with her husband, Darren, and extra-crafty children, Ruby and Oliver.

You can visit her website at littlepincushionstudio.com.